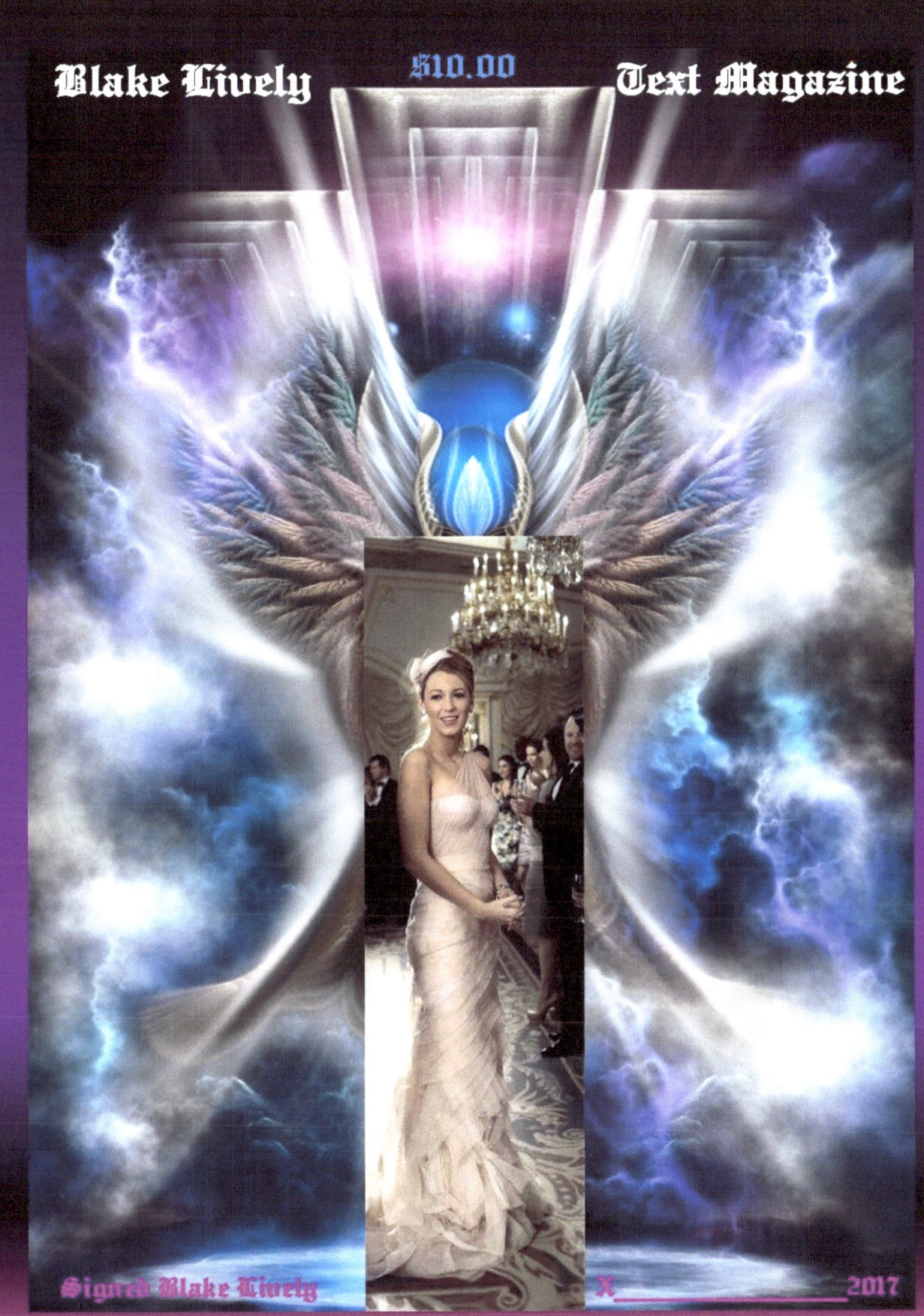

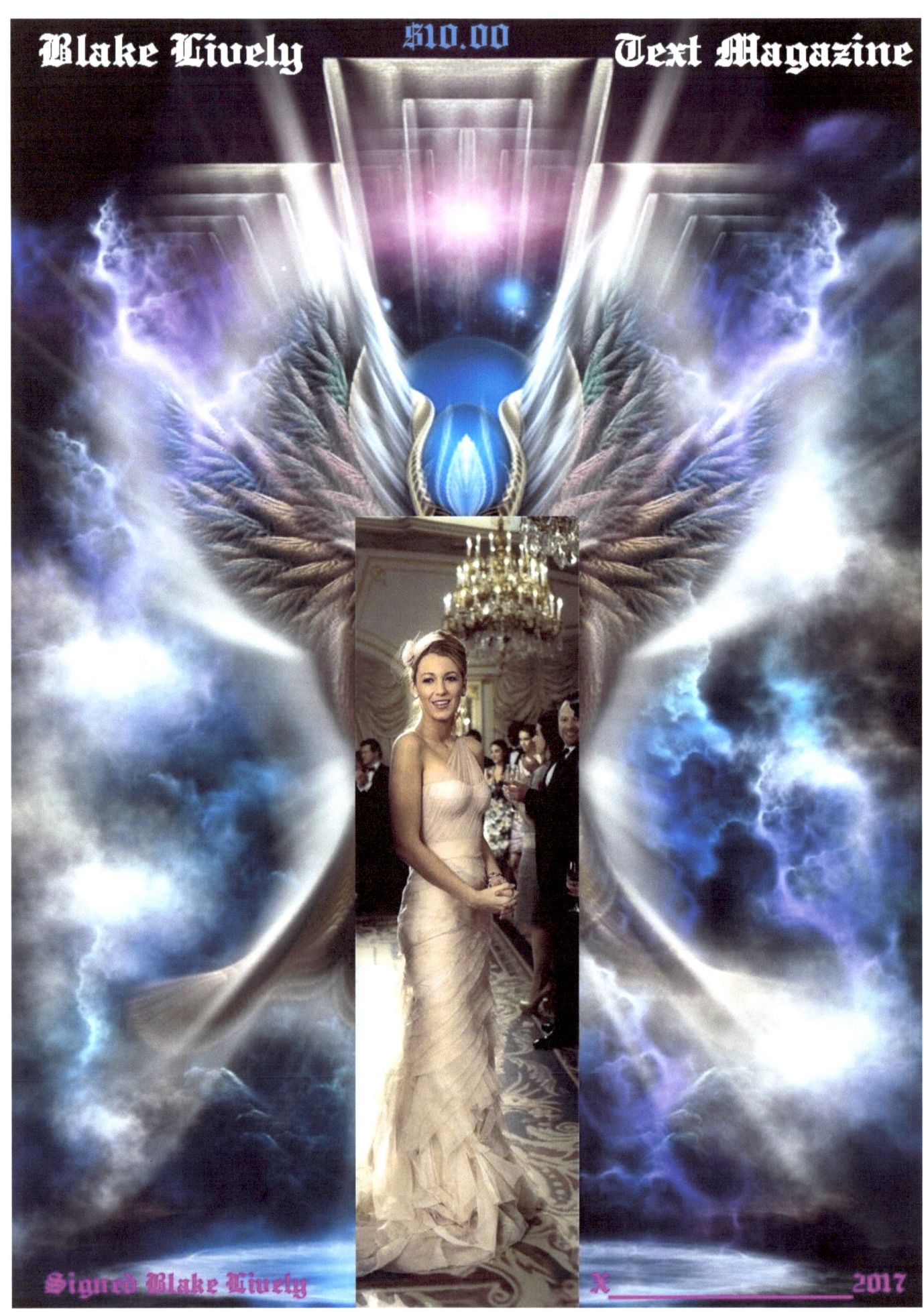

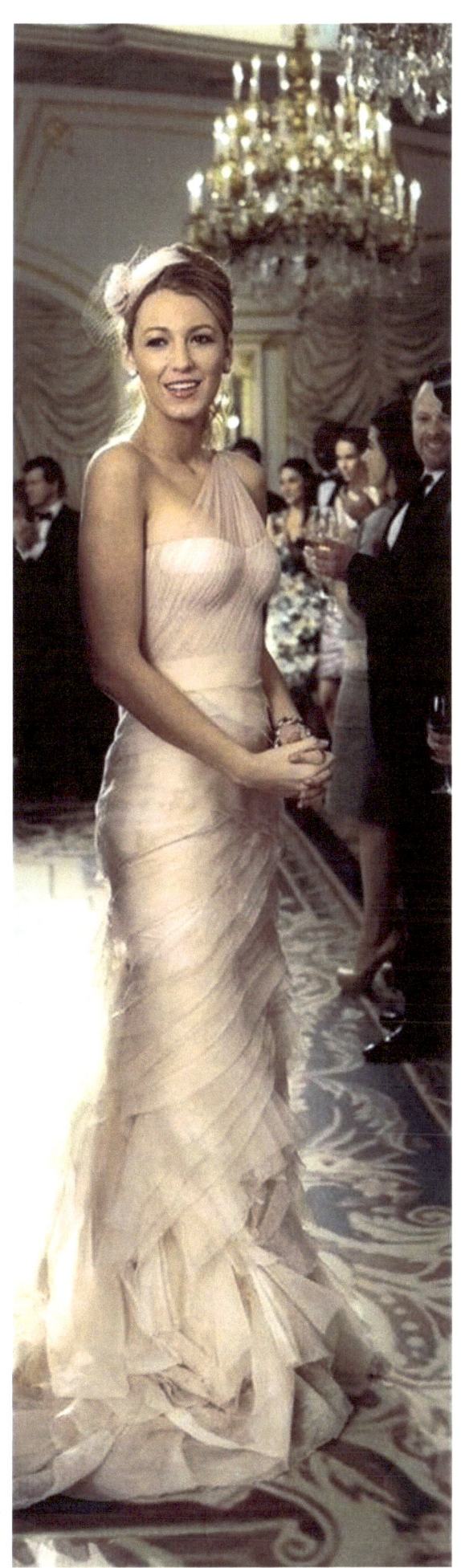

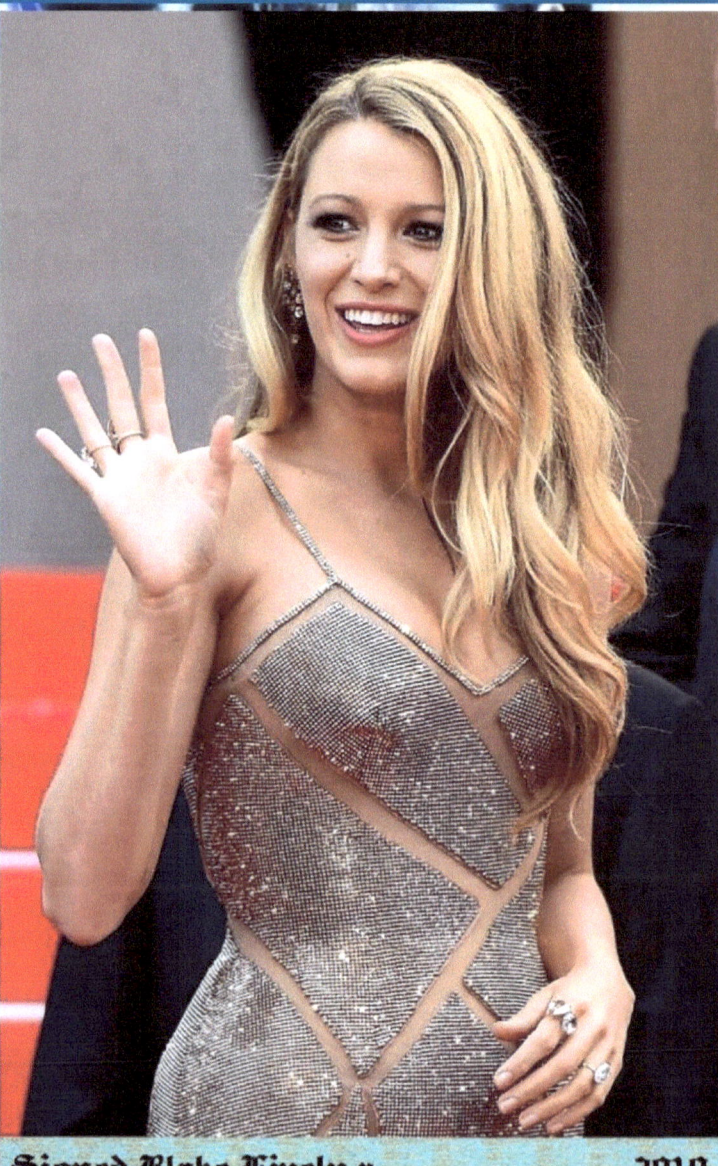

Blake Lively: "Text Magazine" $10

Lavishly Starring Blake Lively

Signed Blake Lively x_____2018

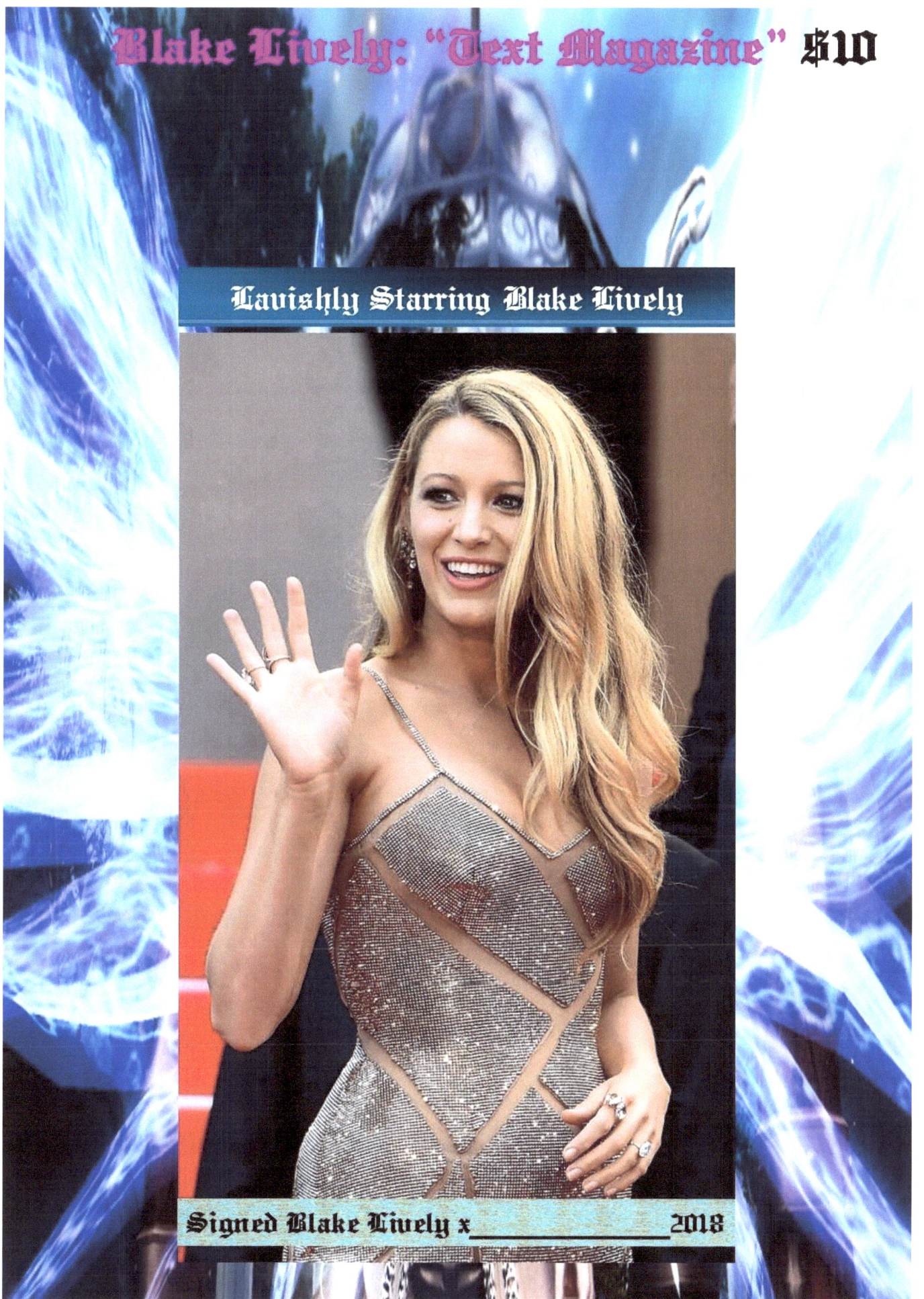

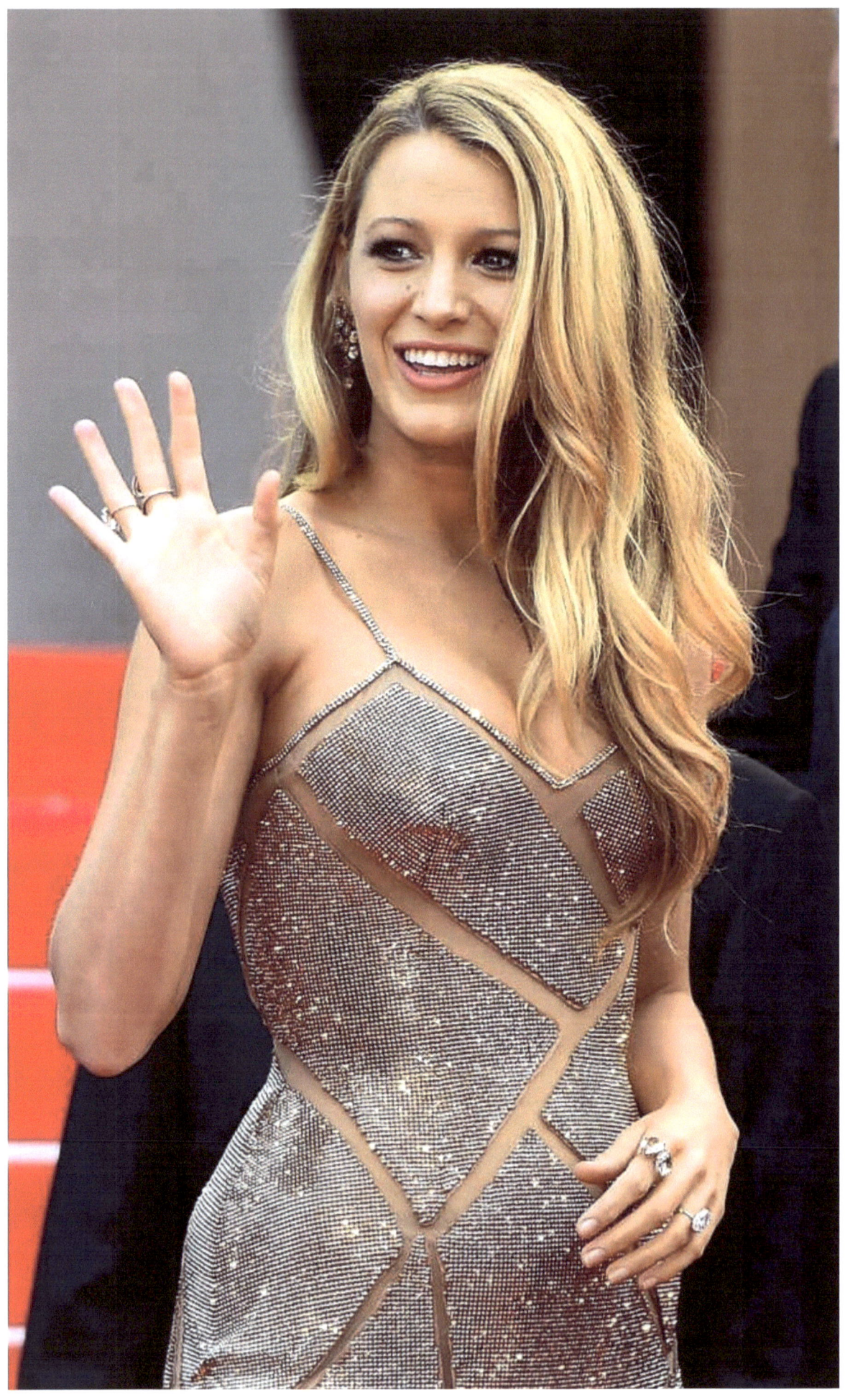

Blake Lively $10.00 "Text Magazine"

Sequestering Blake Lively

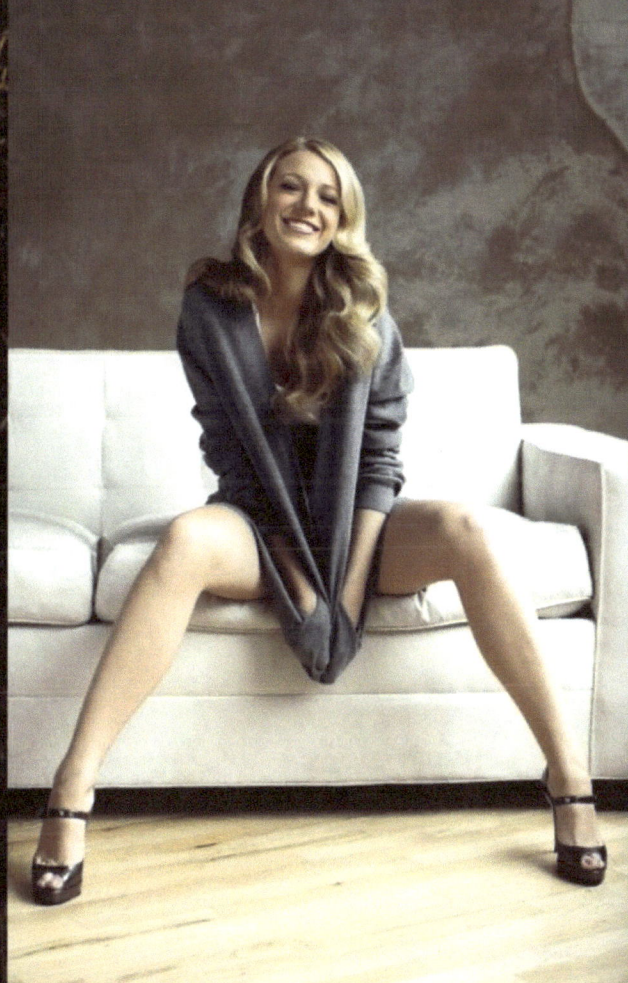

Blake Lively   2018

Blake Lively $10.00 "Text Magazine"

Sequestering Blake Lively

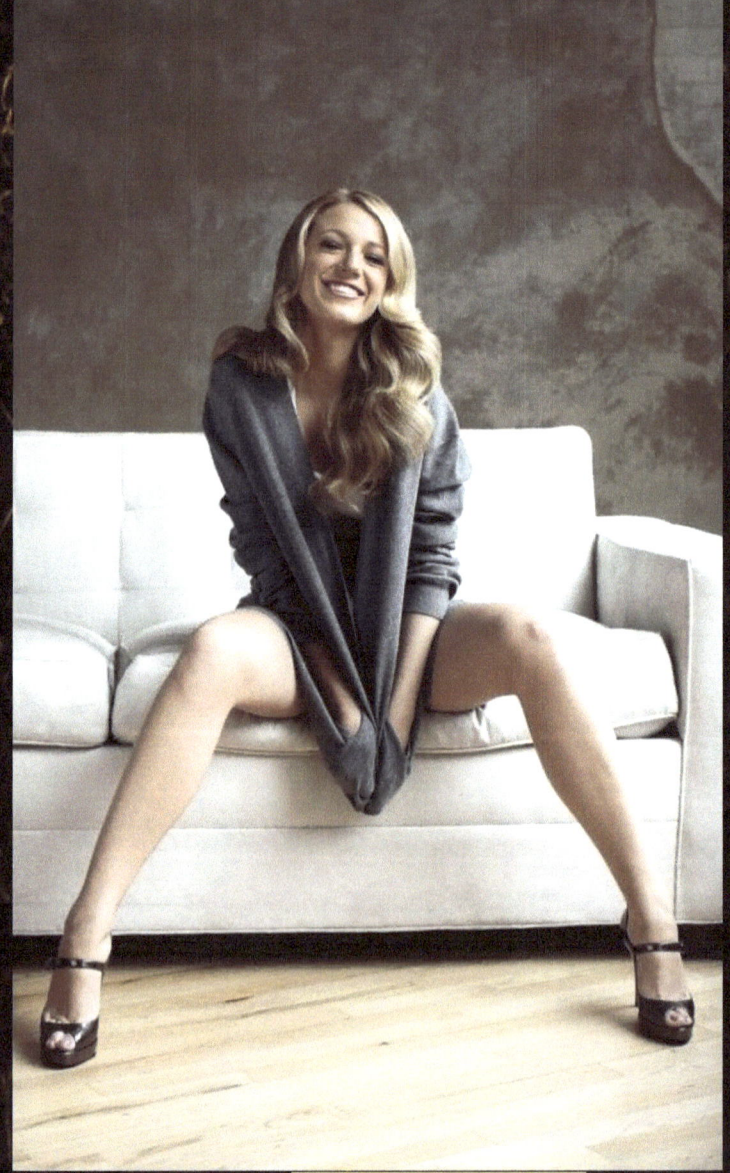

Blake Lively   2013

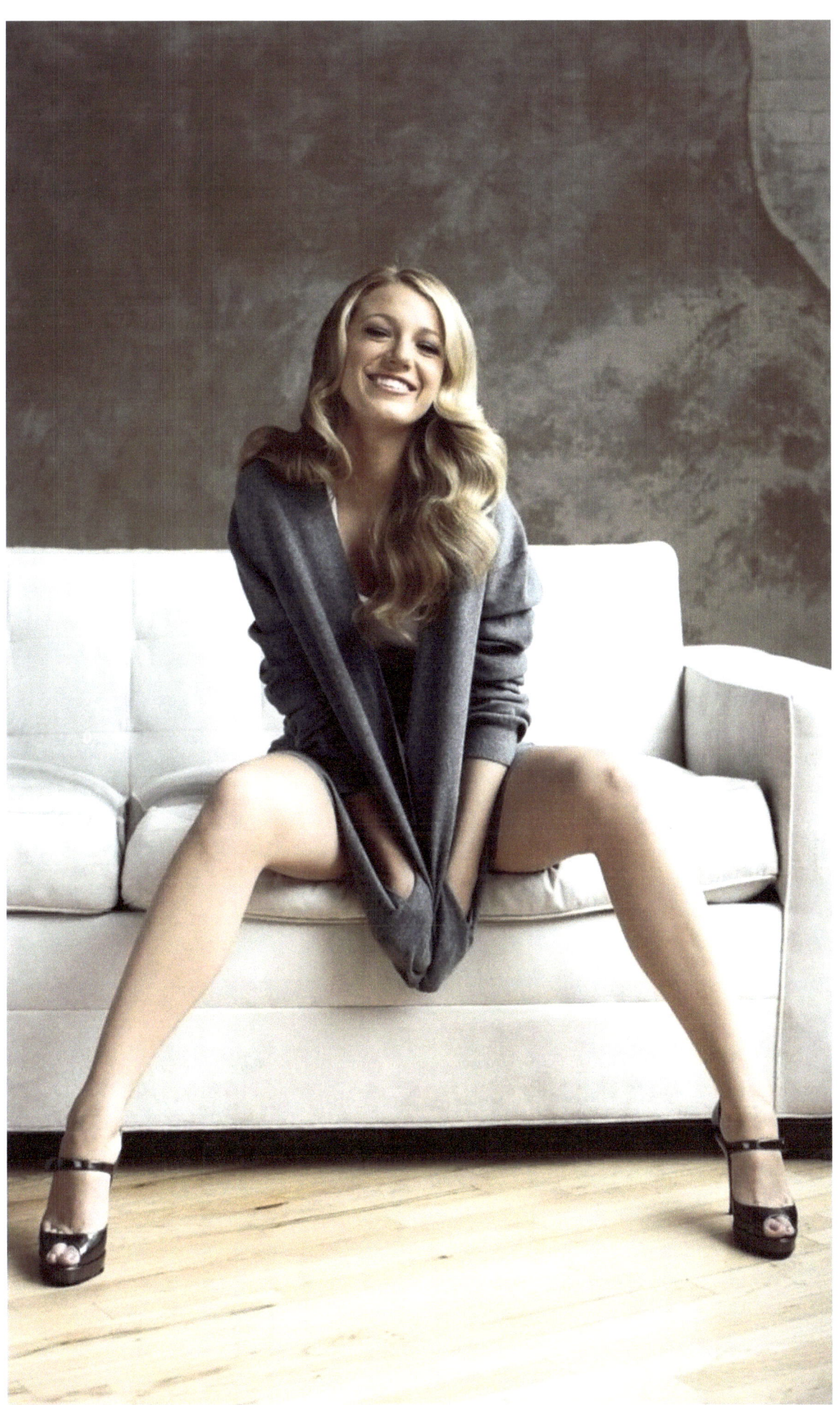

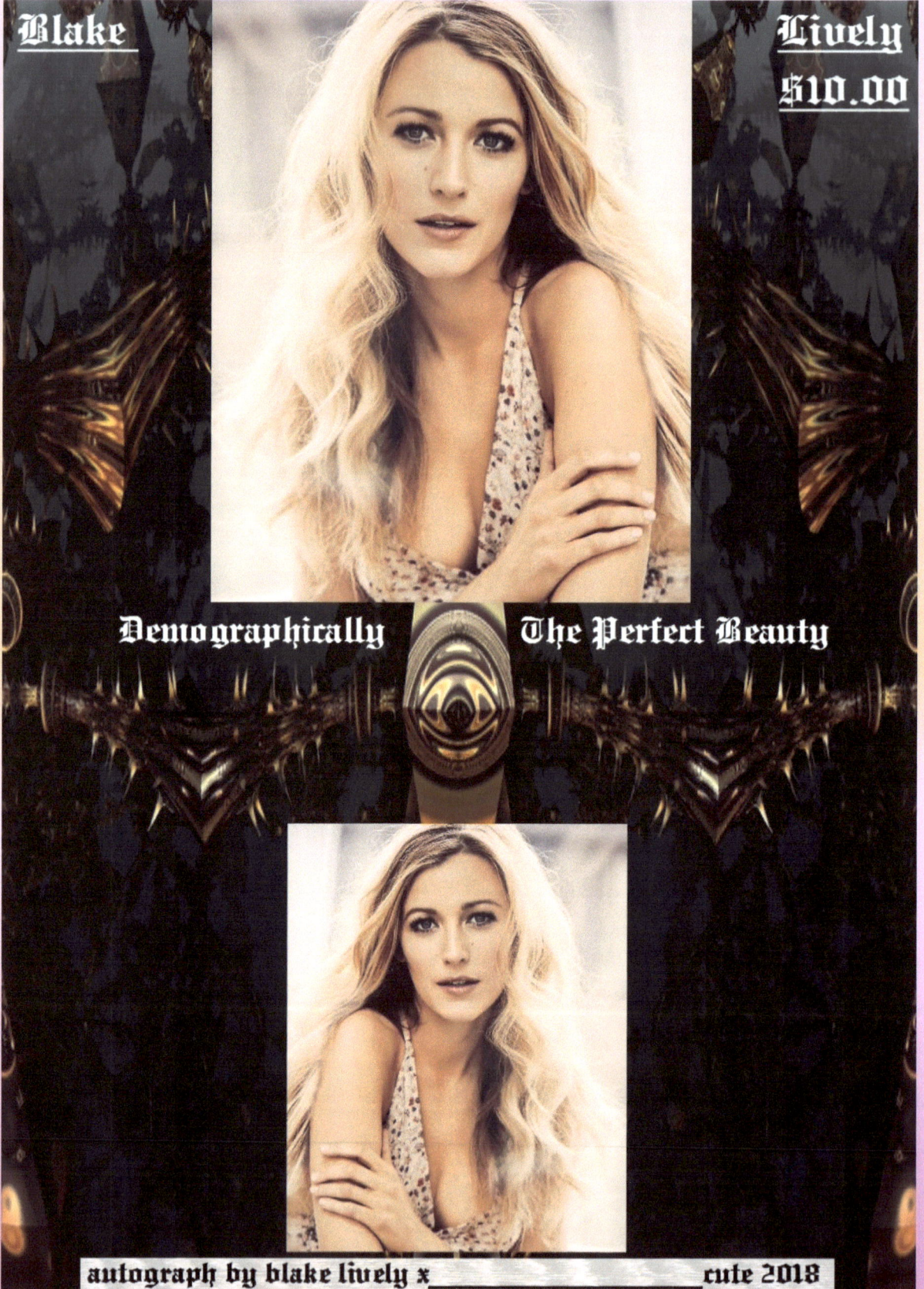

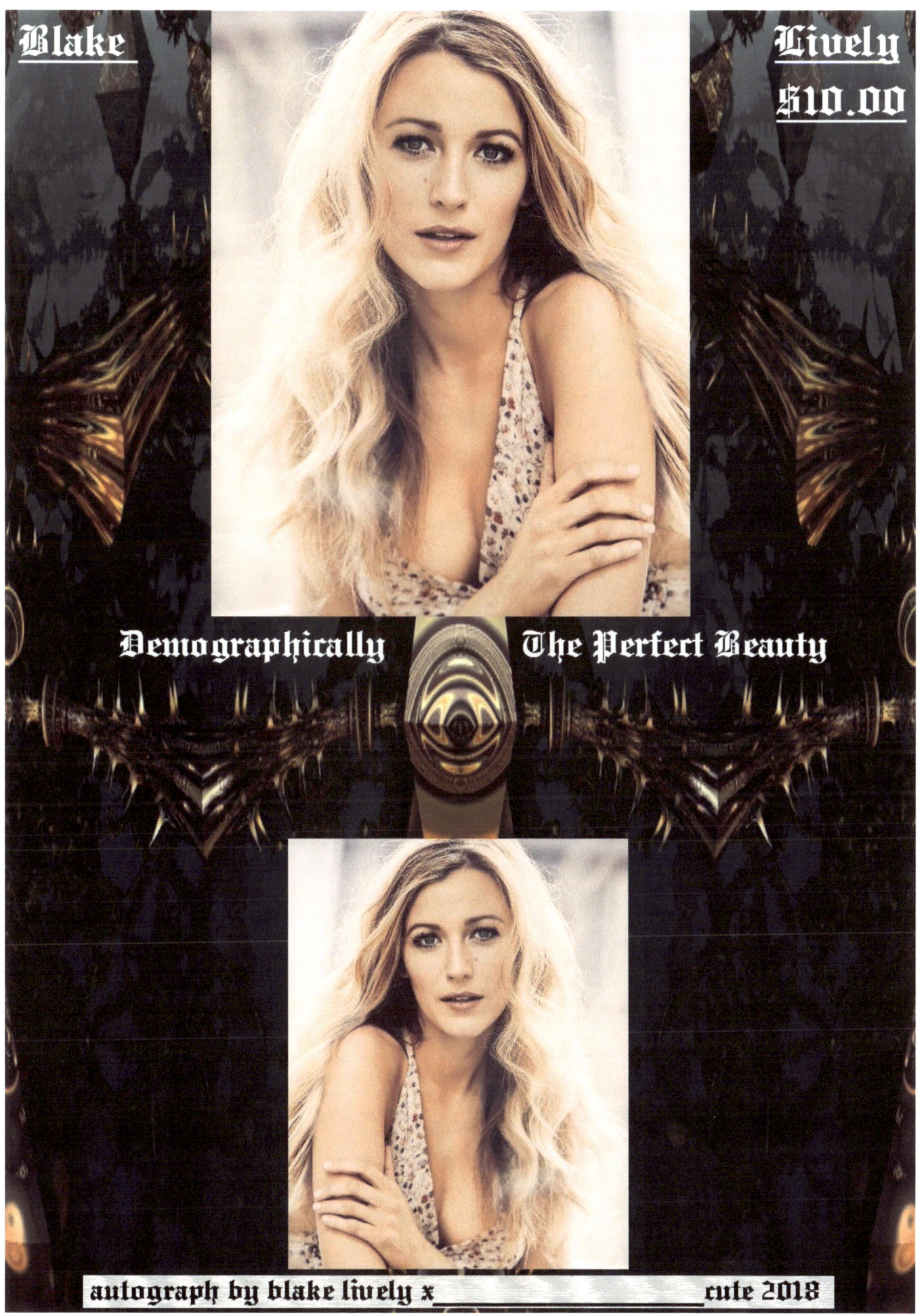

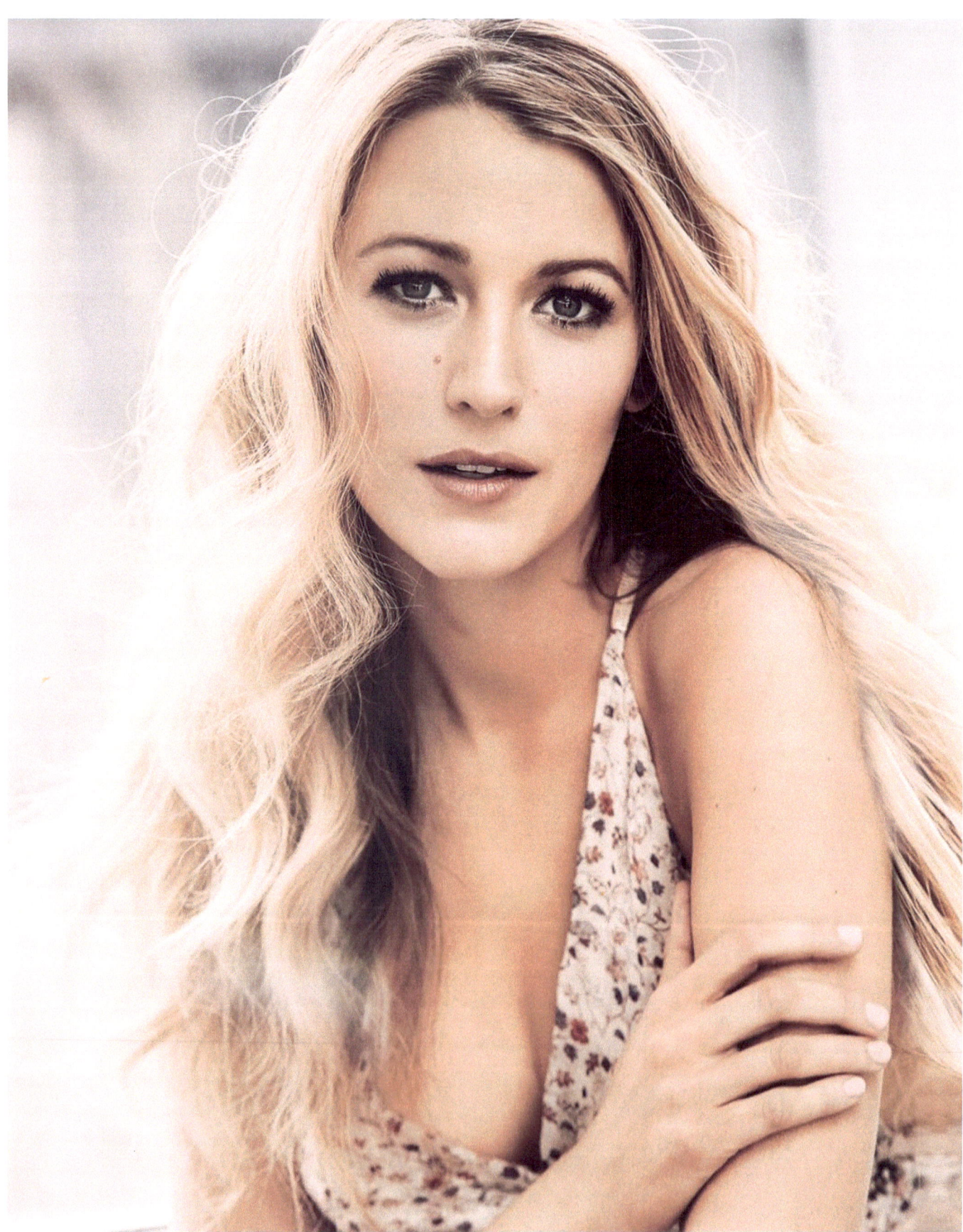

Blake Lively "Text Magazine" $10.00

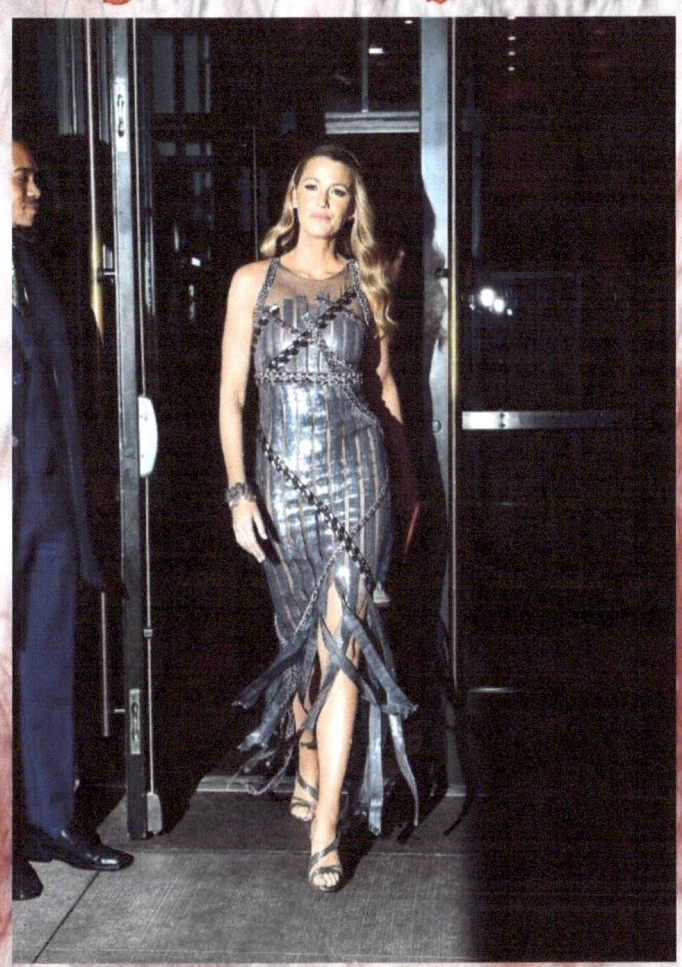

Blake Lively x_____ 2018

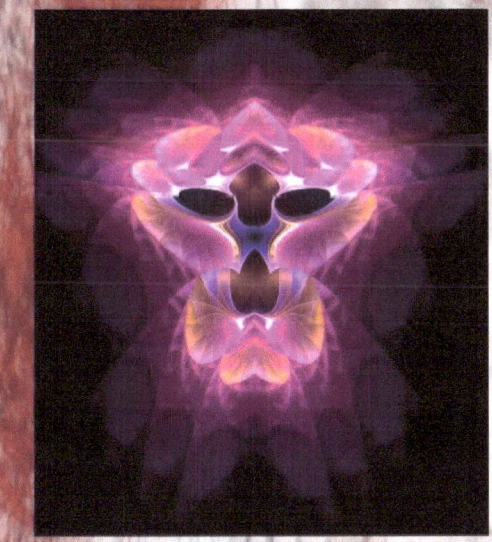 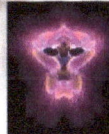 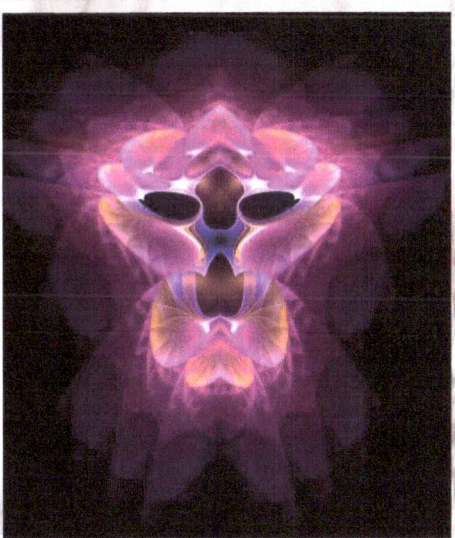
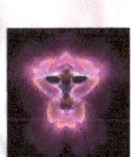
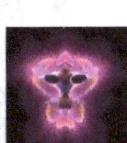

Blake Lively "Text Magazine" $10.00

Blake Lively x_____**2018**

Blake Lively "Text Magazine" $10.00

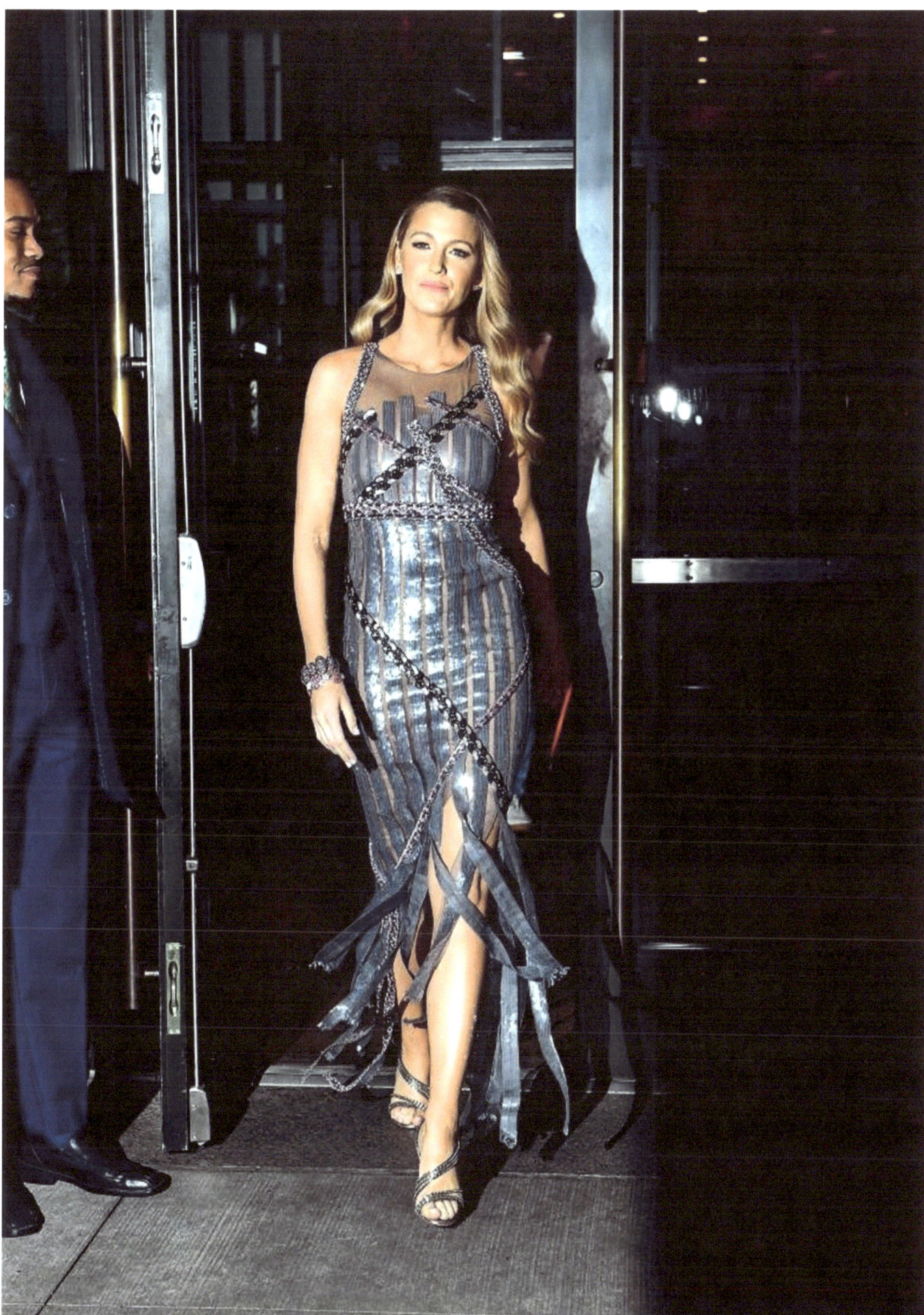

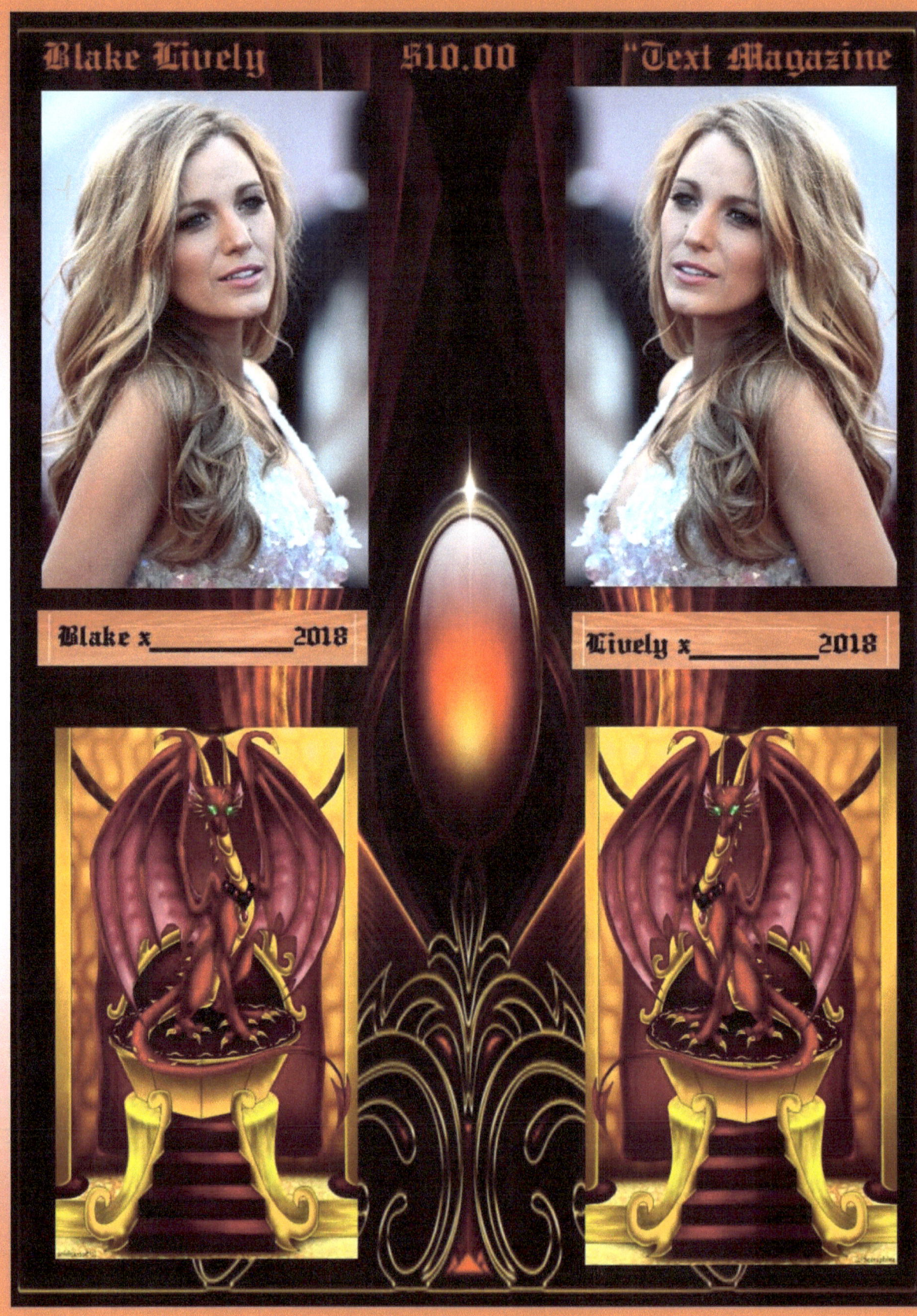

Blake Lively — $10.00 — "Text Magazine

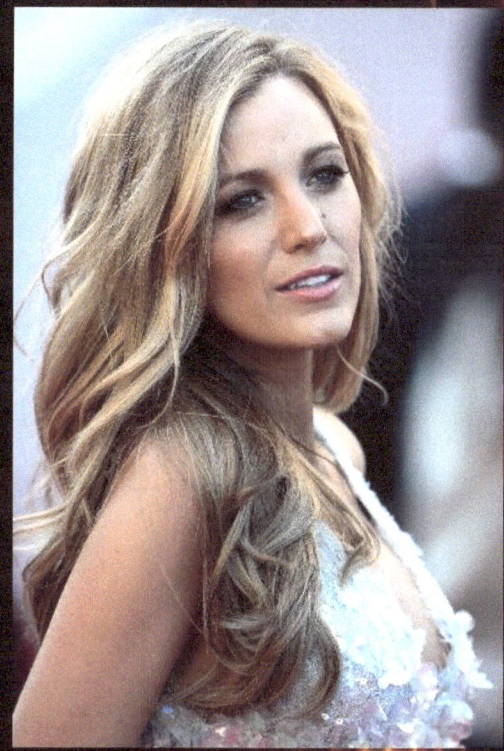

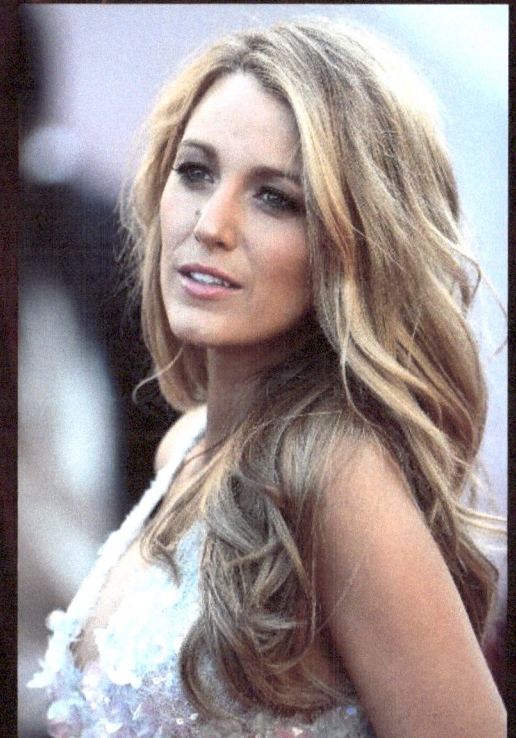

Blake x_____2018

Lively x_____2018

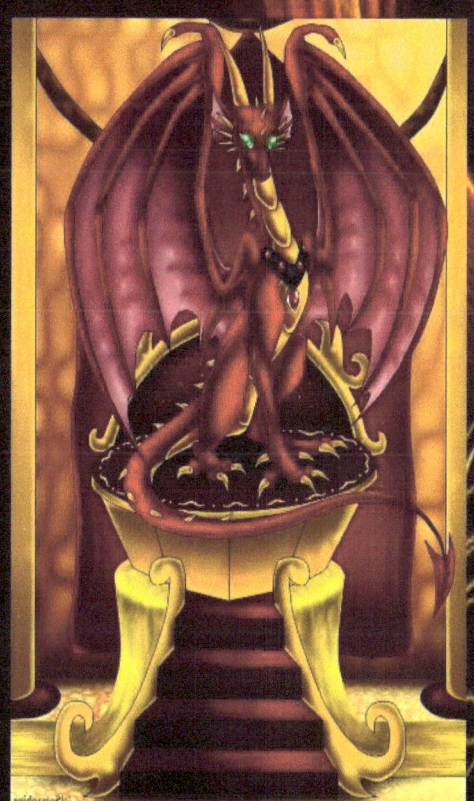

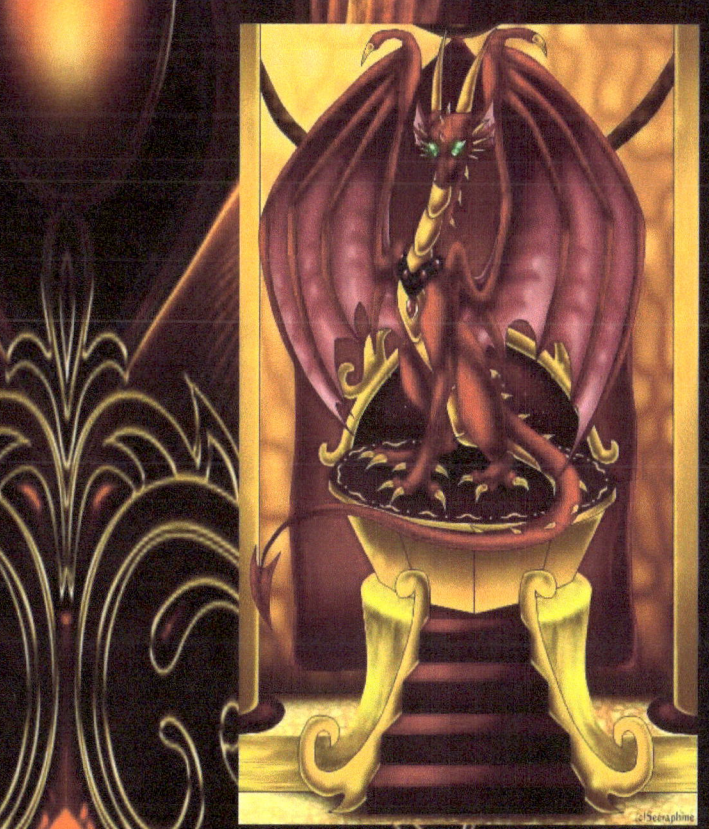

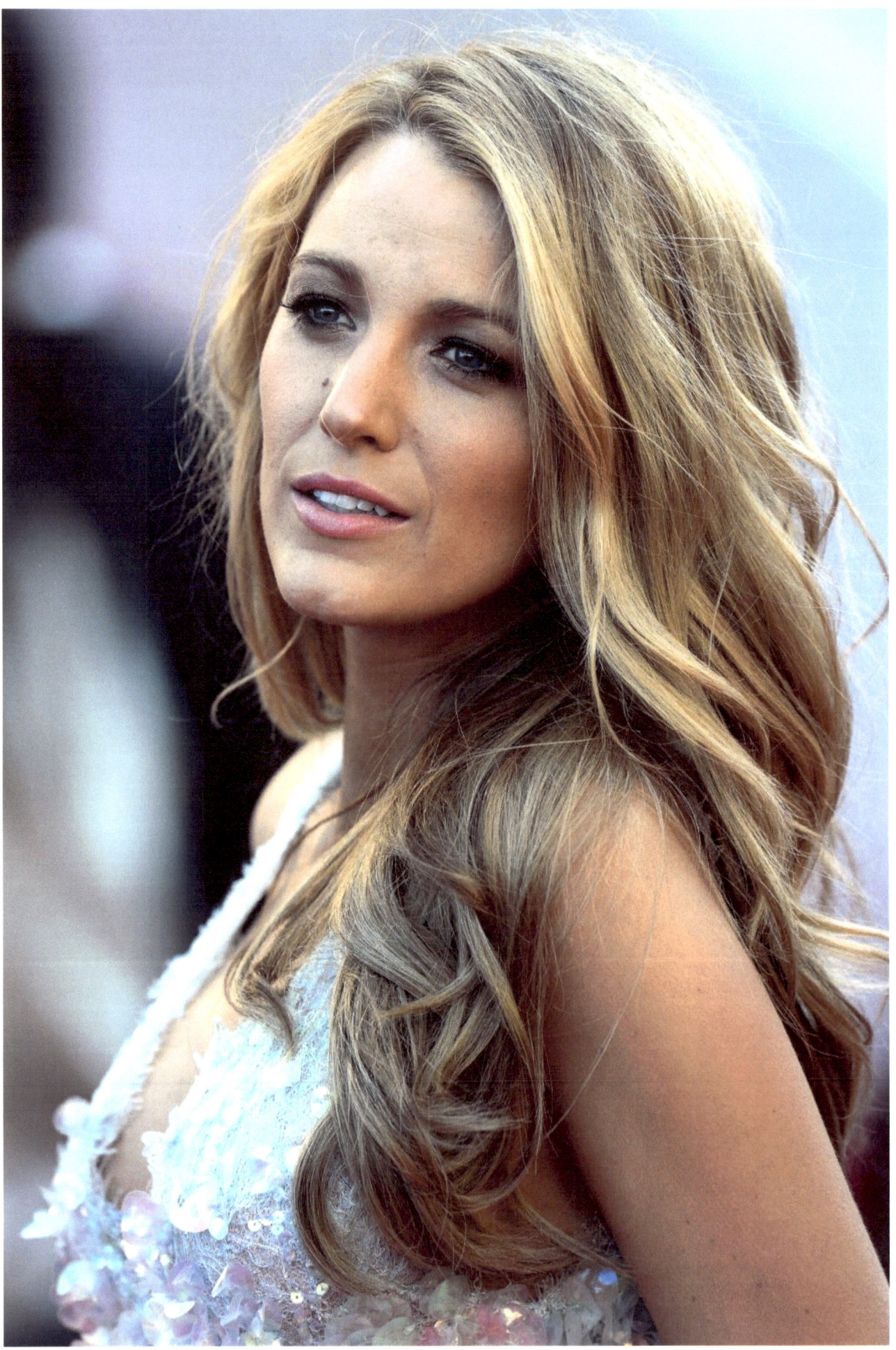

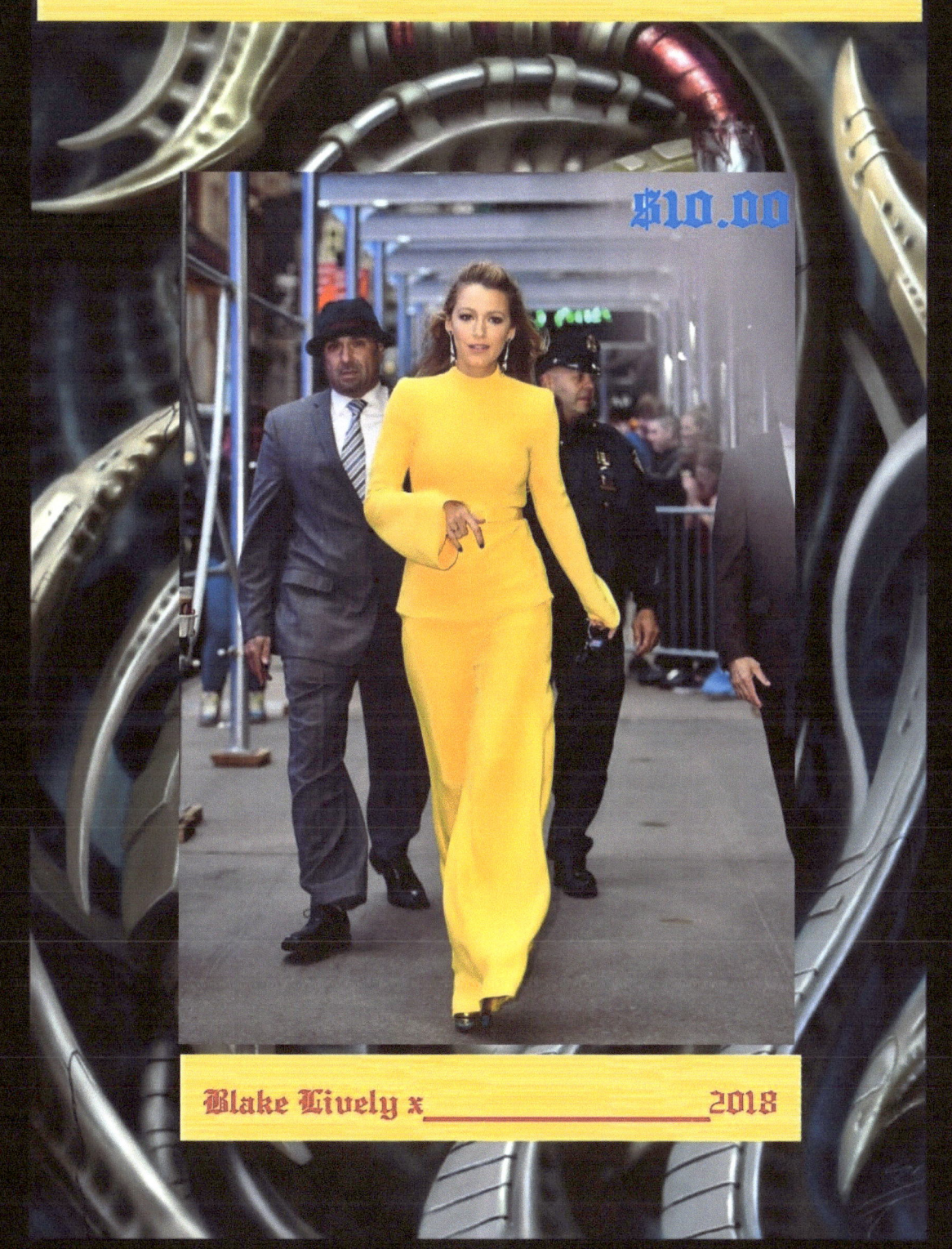

Blake Lively starring in "Text Magazine"

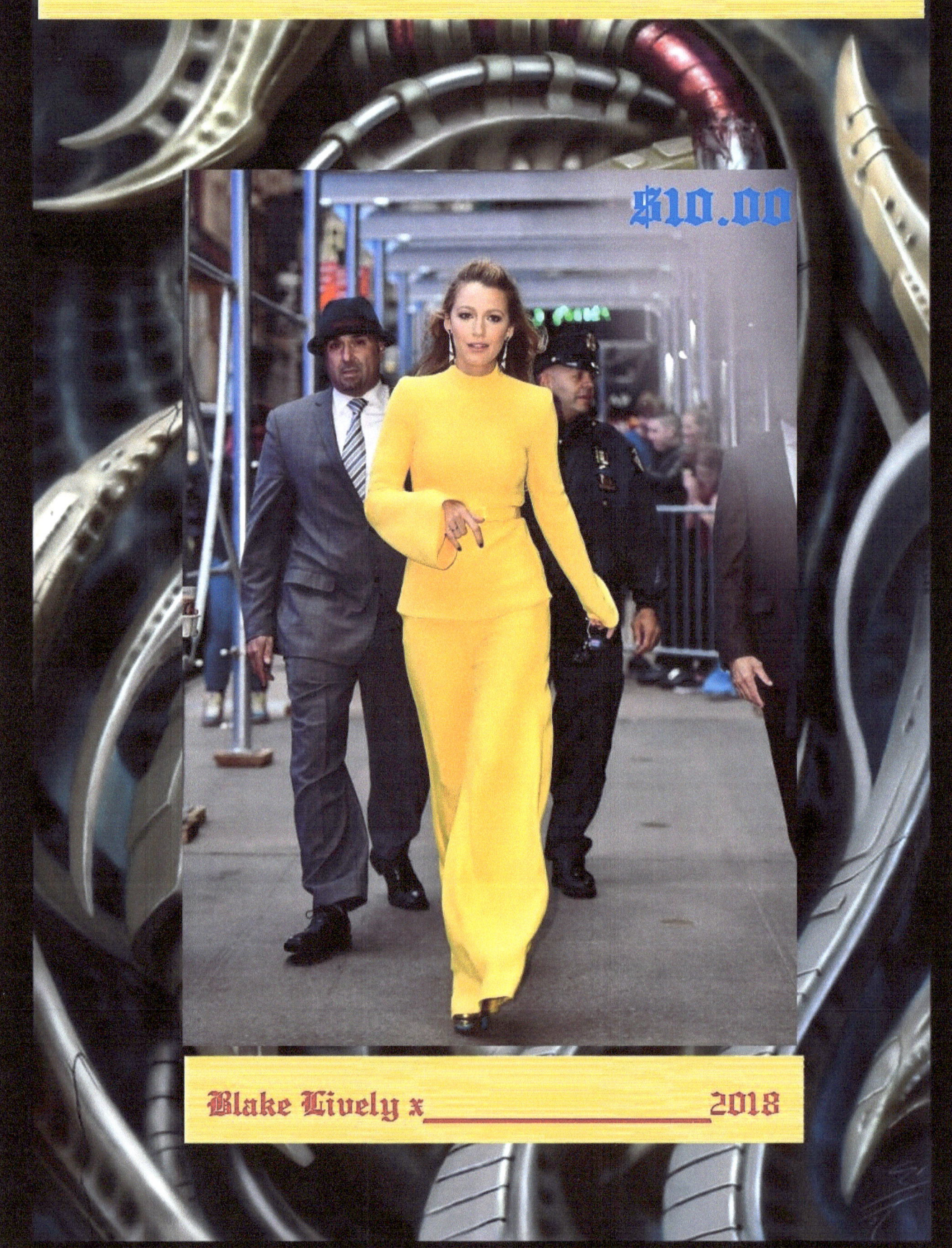

$10.00

Blake Lively x_____ 2018

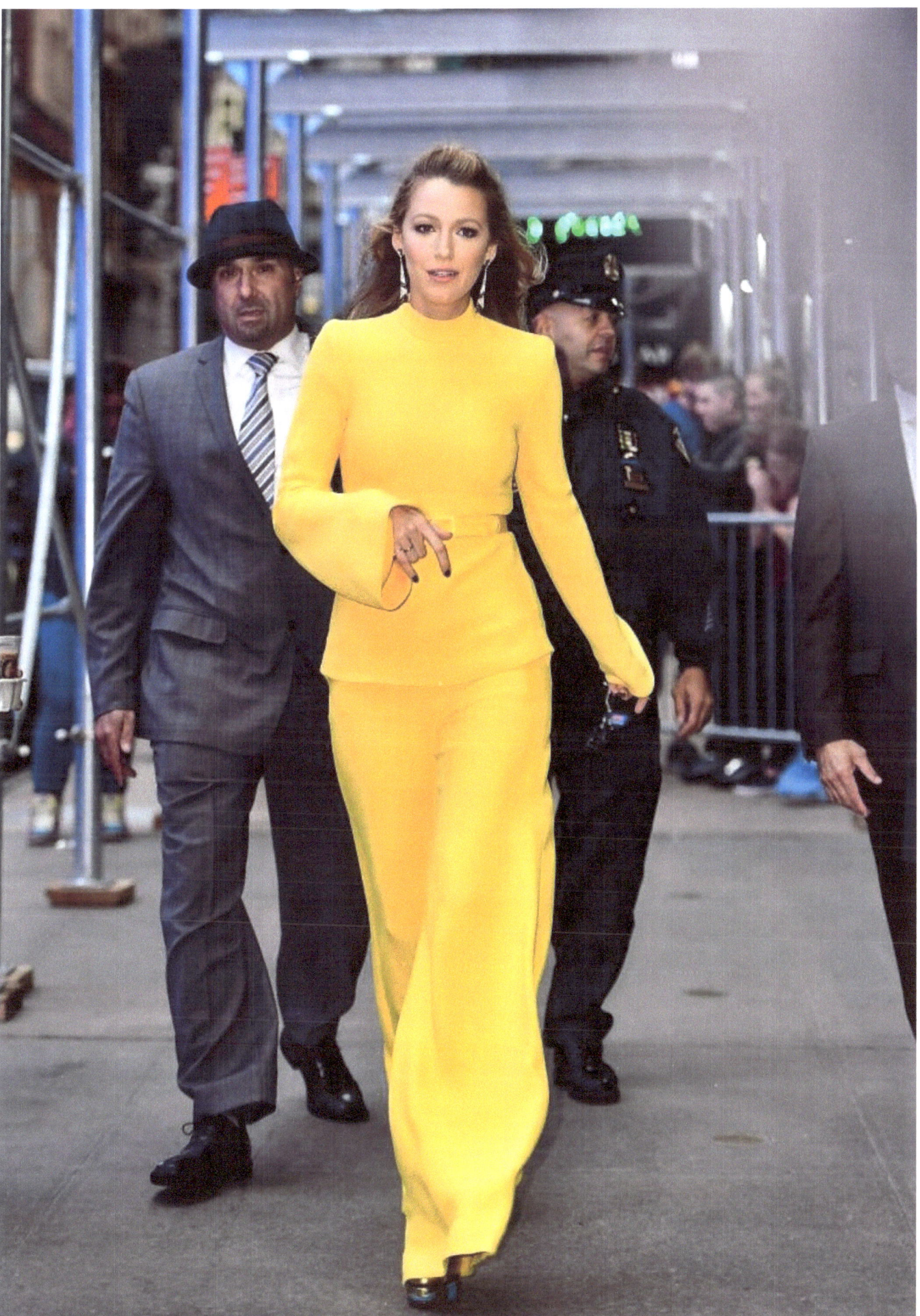

Blake Lively "Text Magazine" $10.00

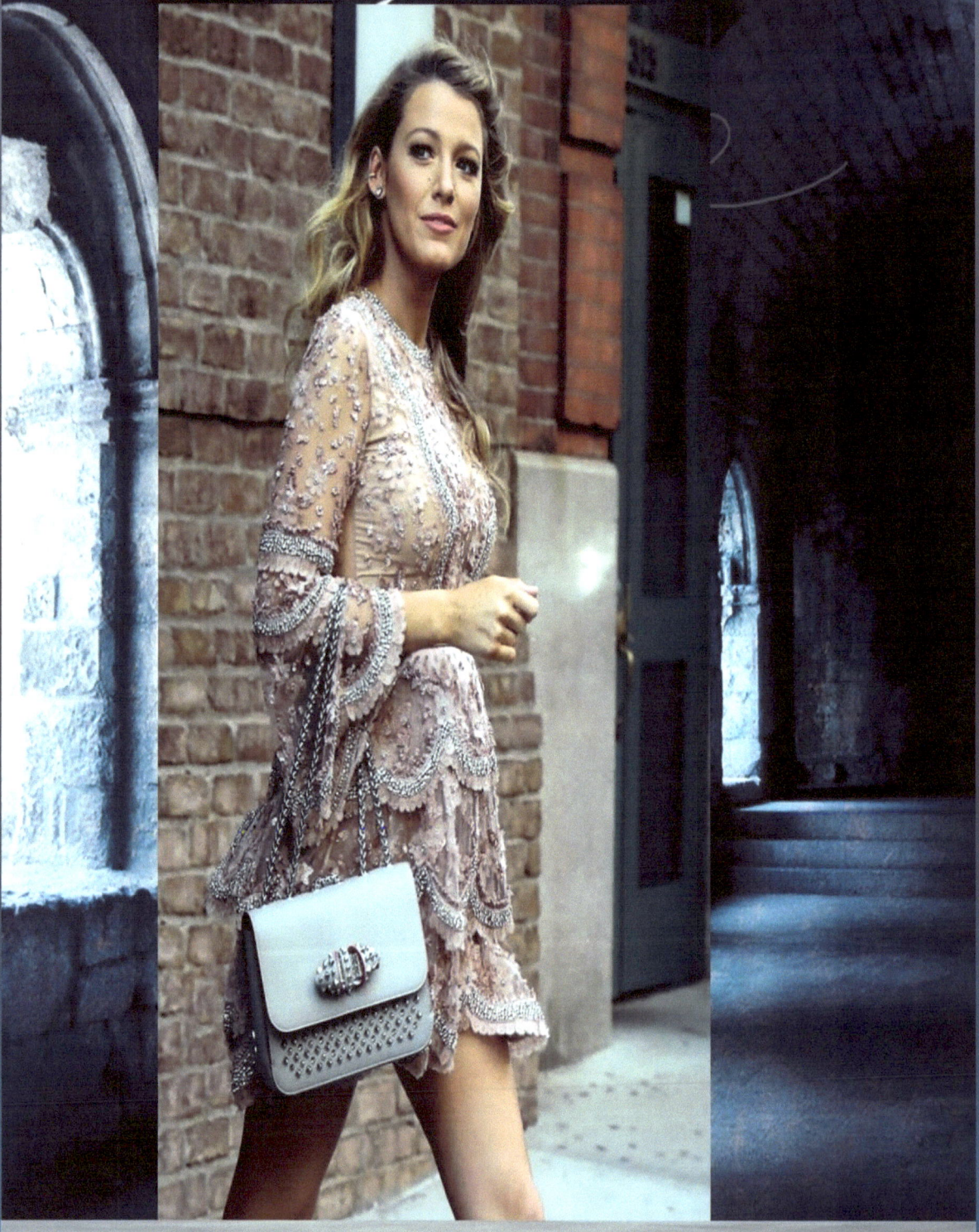

The Castle of Blake Lively x_____ 2018

Blake Lively "Text Magazine" $10.00

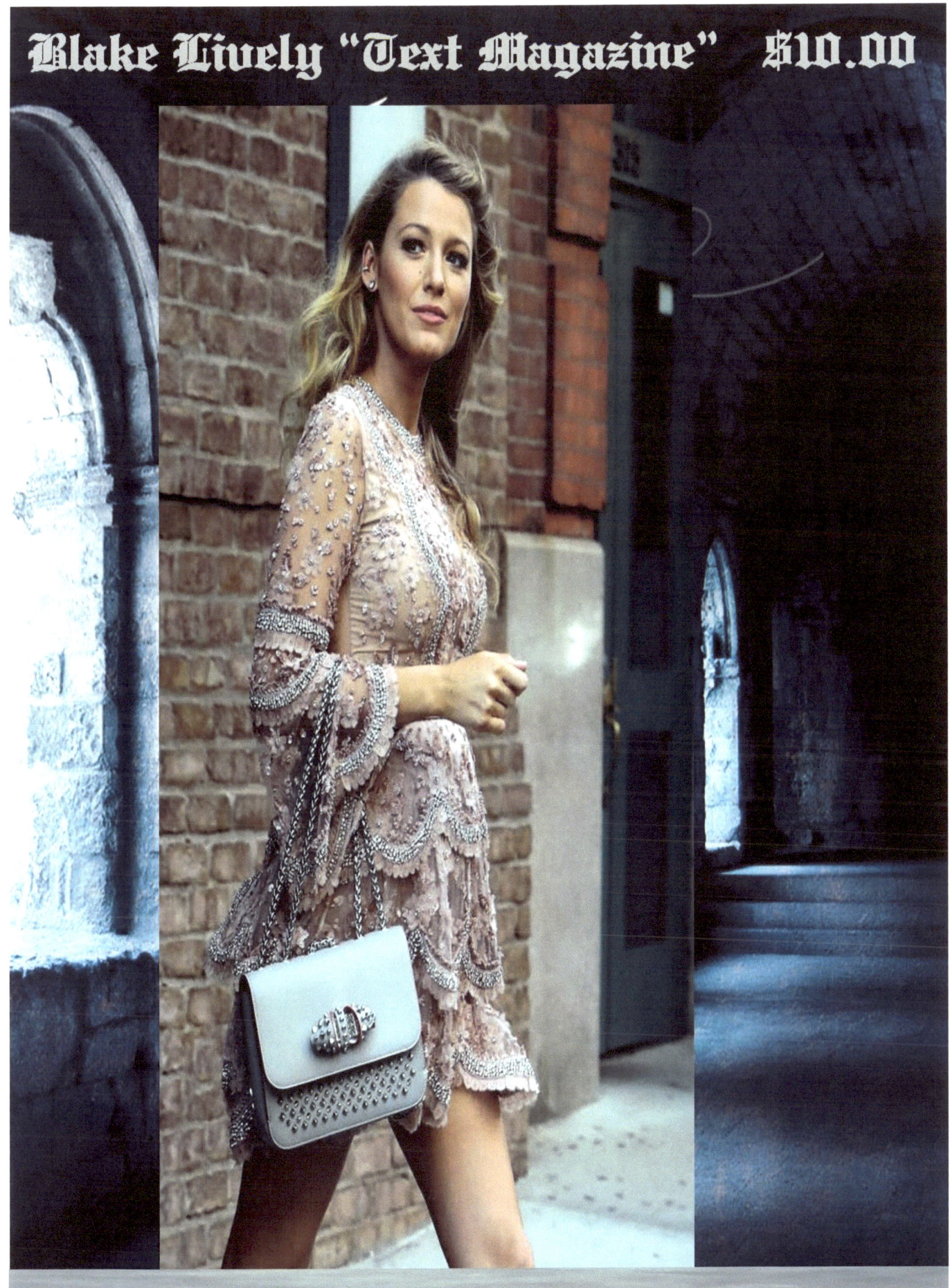

The Castle of Blake Lively x_____ 2018

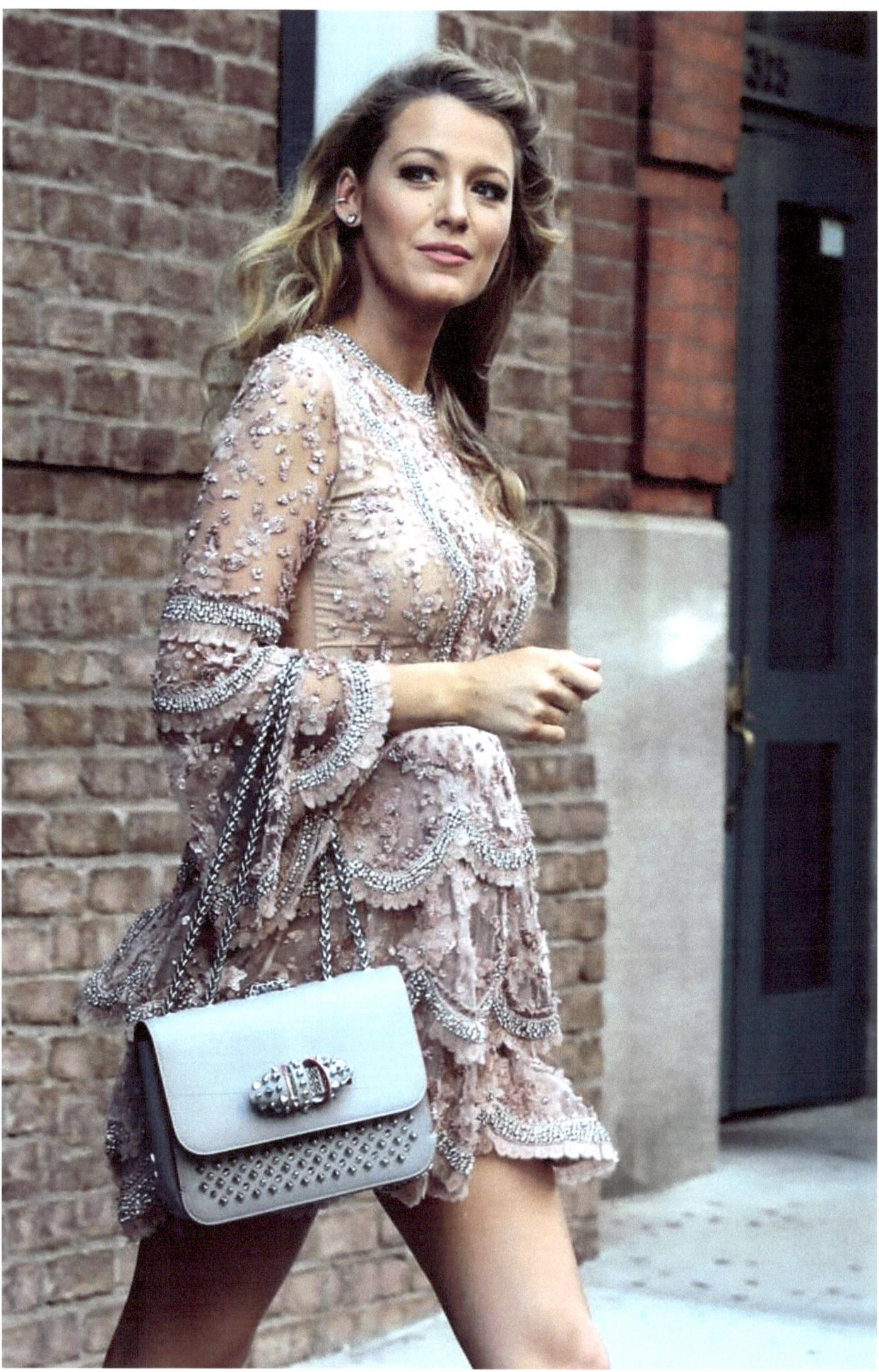

Blake Lively "Text Magazine" $10.00

Captivating Ms. Blake Lively

| Blake Lively | x_____ | Blue 2018 |

The subtle touch of thee glamourous woman of fame and beauty Blake Lively dp

Blake Lively "Text Magazine" $10.00

Captivating Ms. Blake Lively

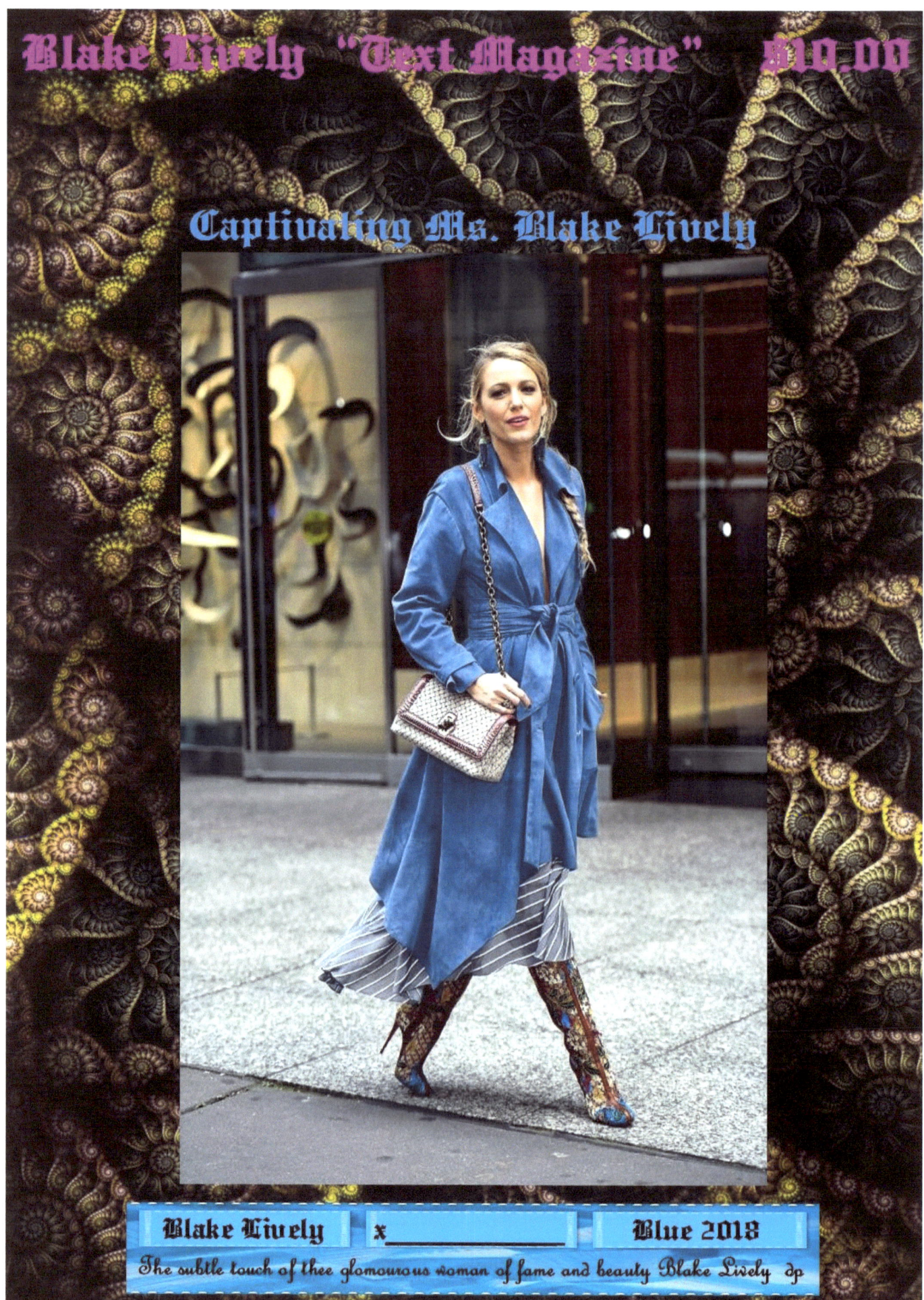

Blake Lively   x_____   **Blue 2018**

The subtle touch of thee glamourous woman of fame and beauty Blake Lively dp

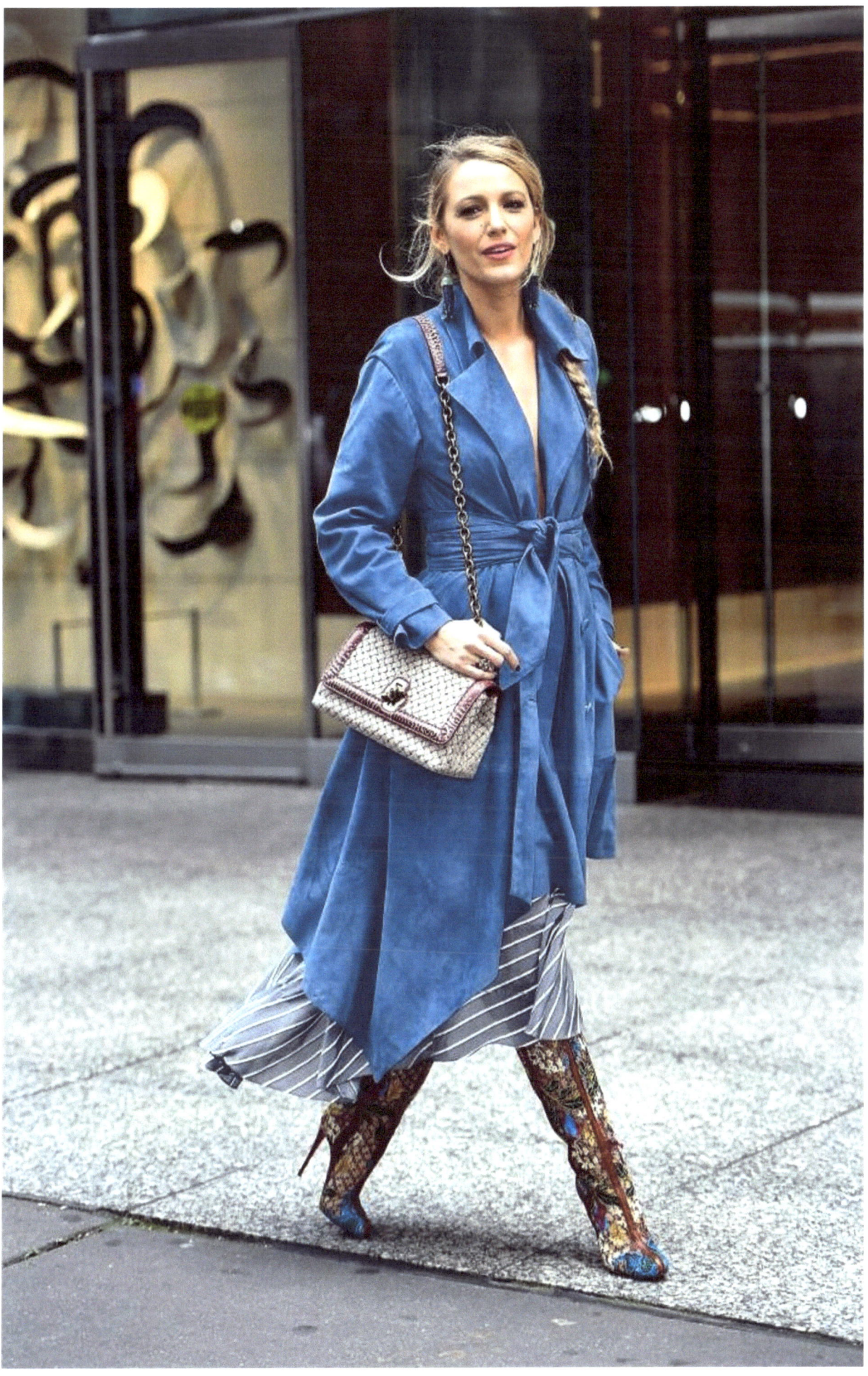

Blake Lively "Text Magazine" $10.00

Bedazzling Blake Lively

Signed: Blake Lively x_____ 2018

the dancing footsteps of the nude goddess make room for love dp

Blake Lively "Text Magazine" $10.00

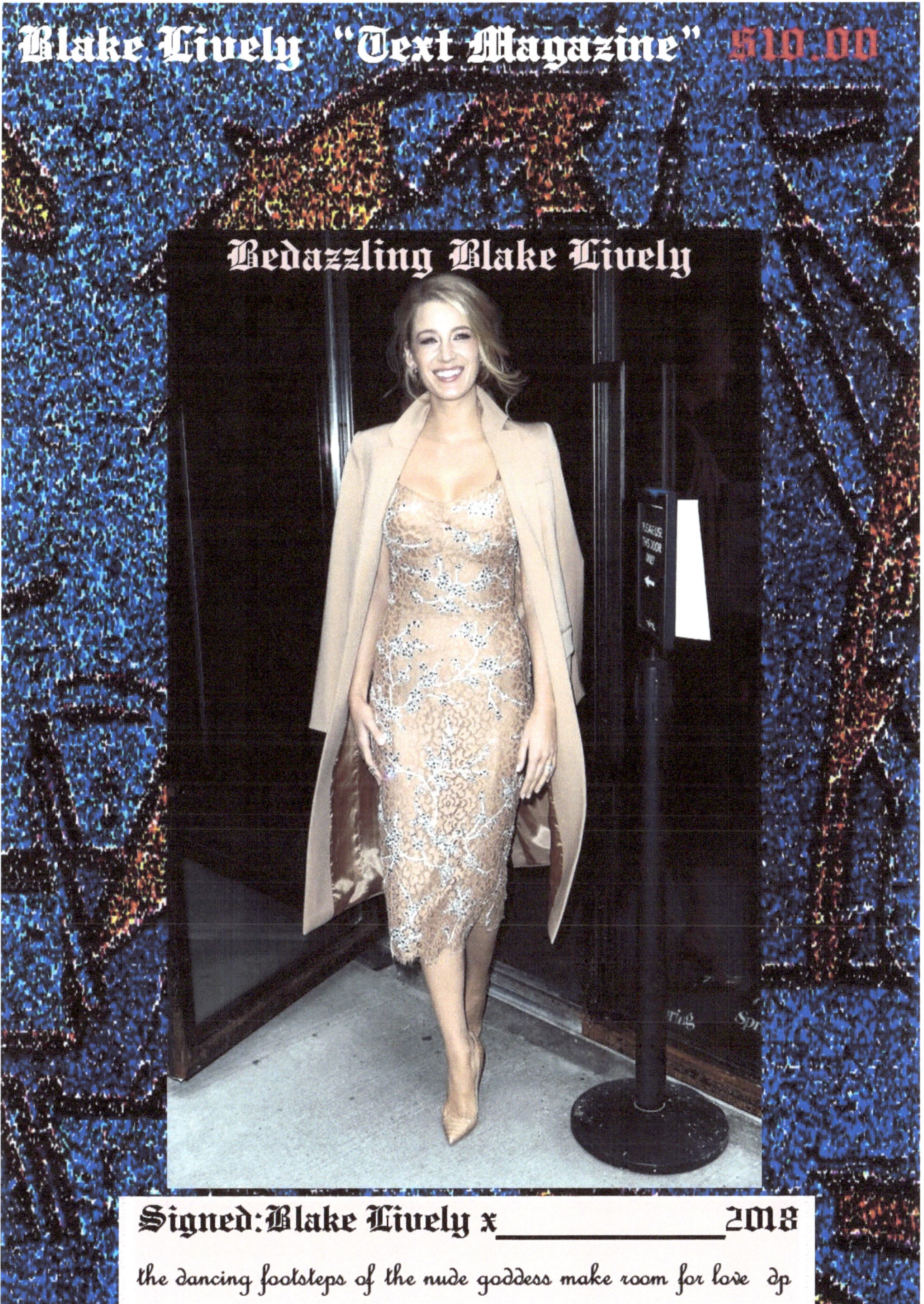

Bedazzling Blake Lively

Signed: Blake Lively x_____ 2018

the dancing footsteps of the nude goddess make room for love dp

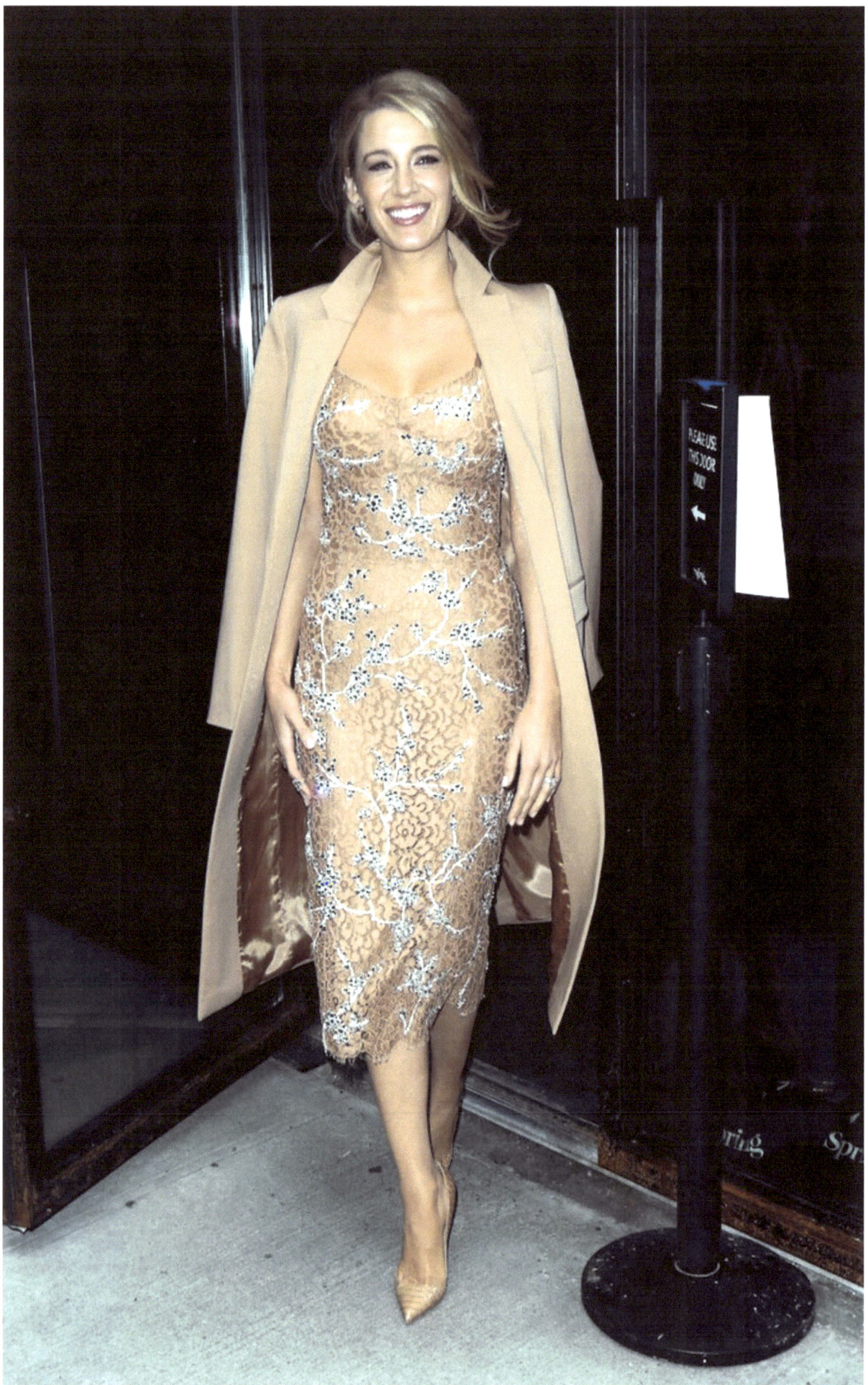

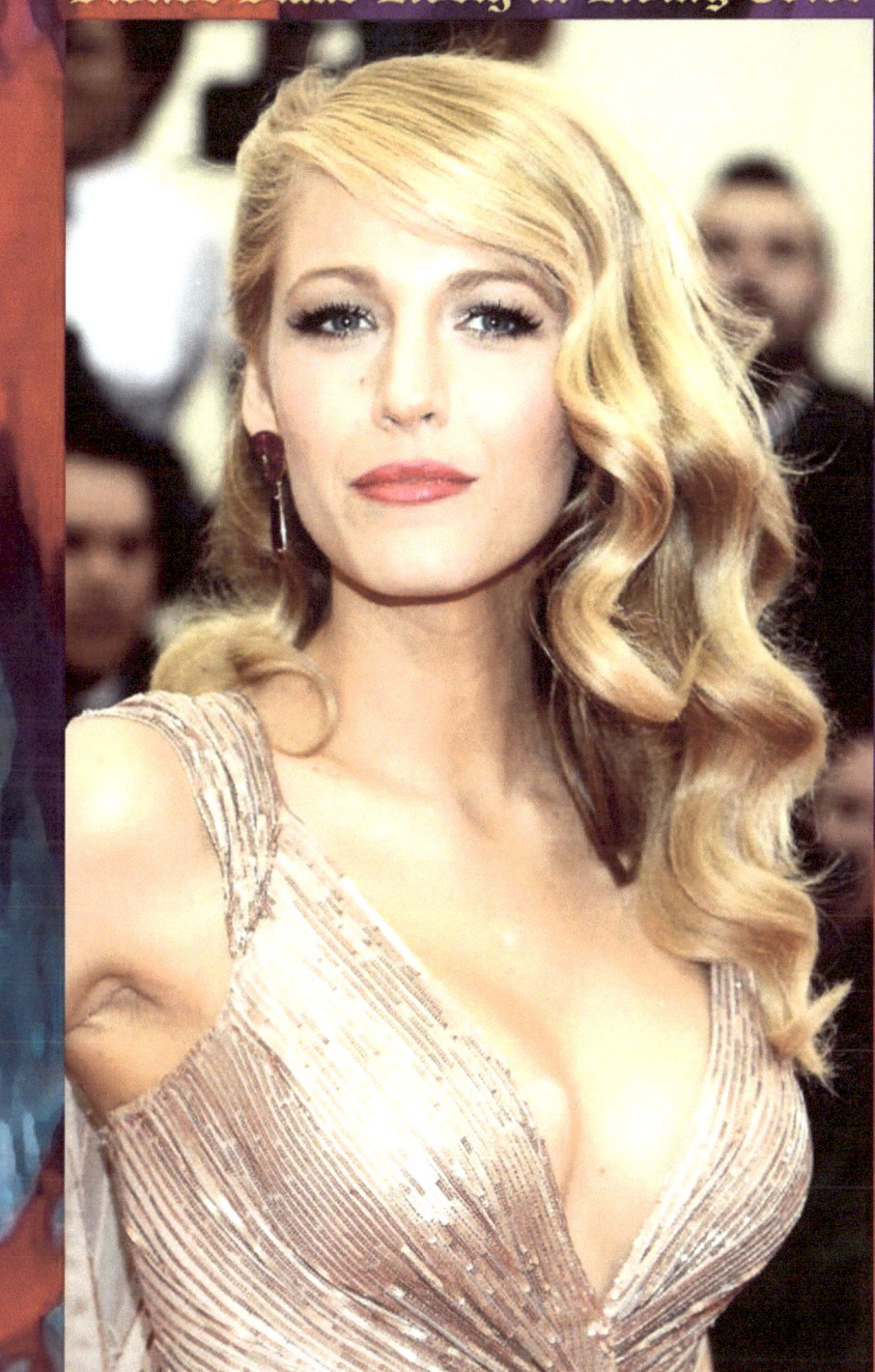

Blake Lively "Text Magazine" $10.00

Blonde Blake Lively in Living Color

Autographed by: Blake Lively x   2018

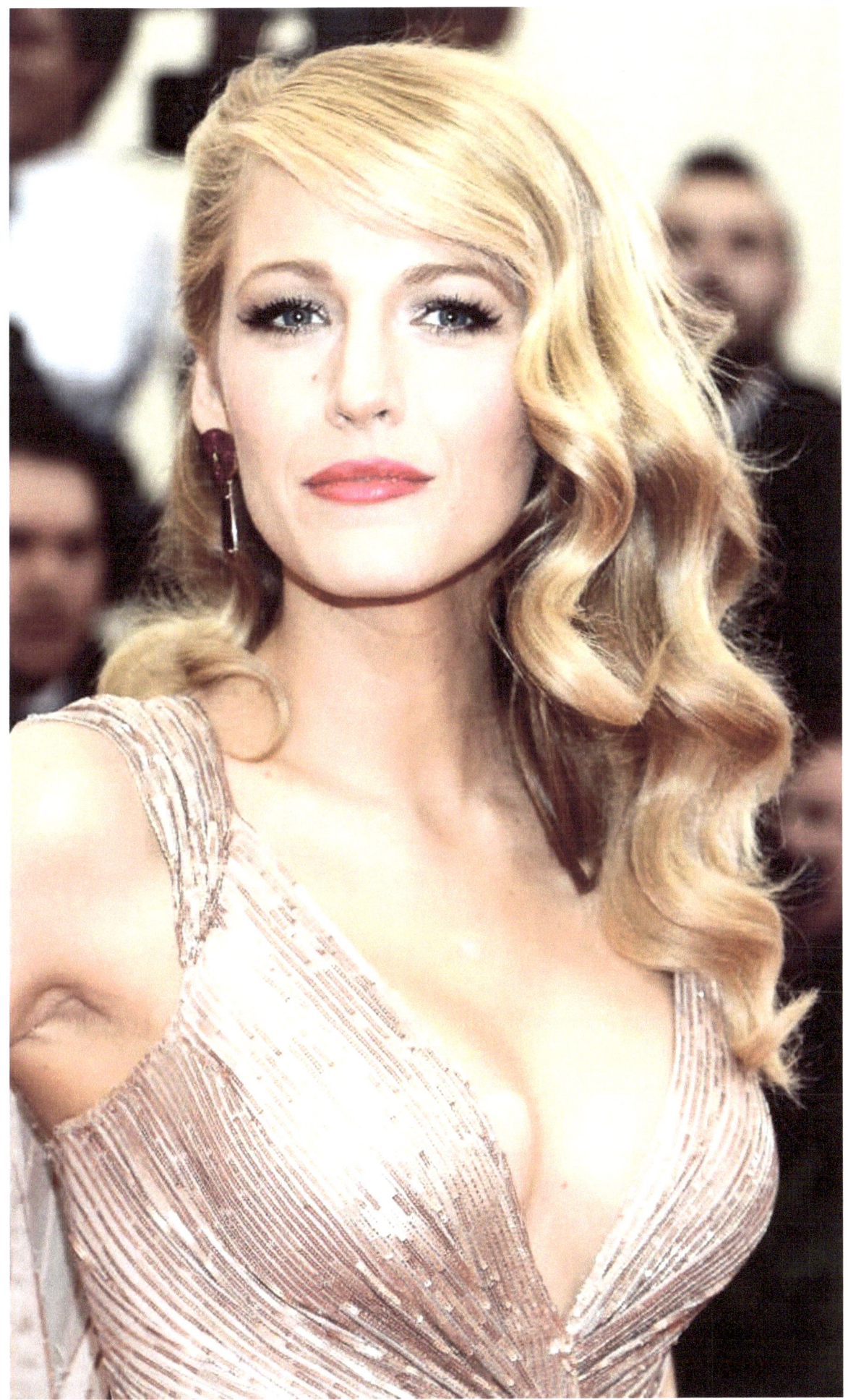

Blake Lively   "Text Magazine" $10.00

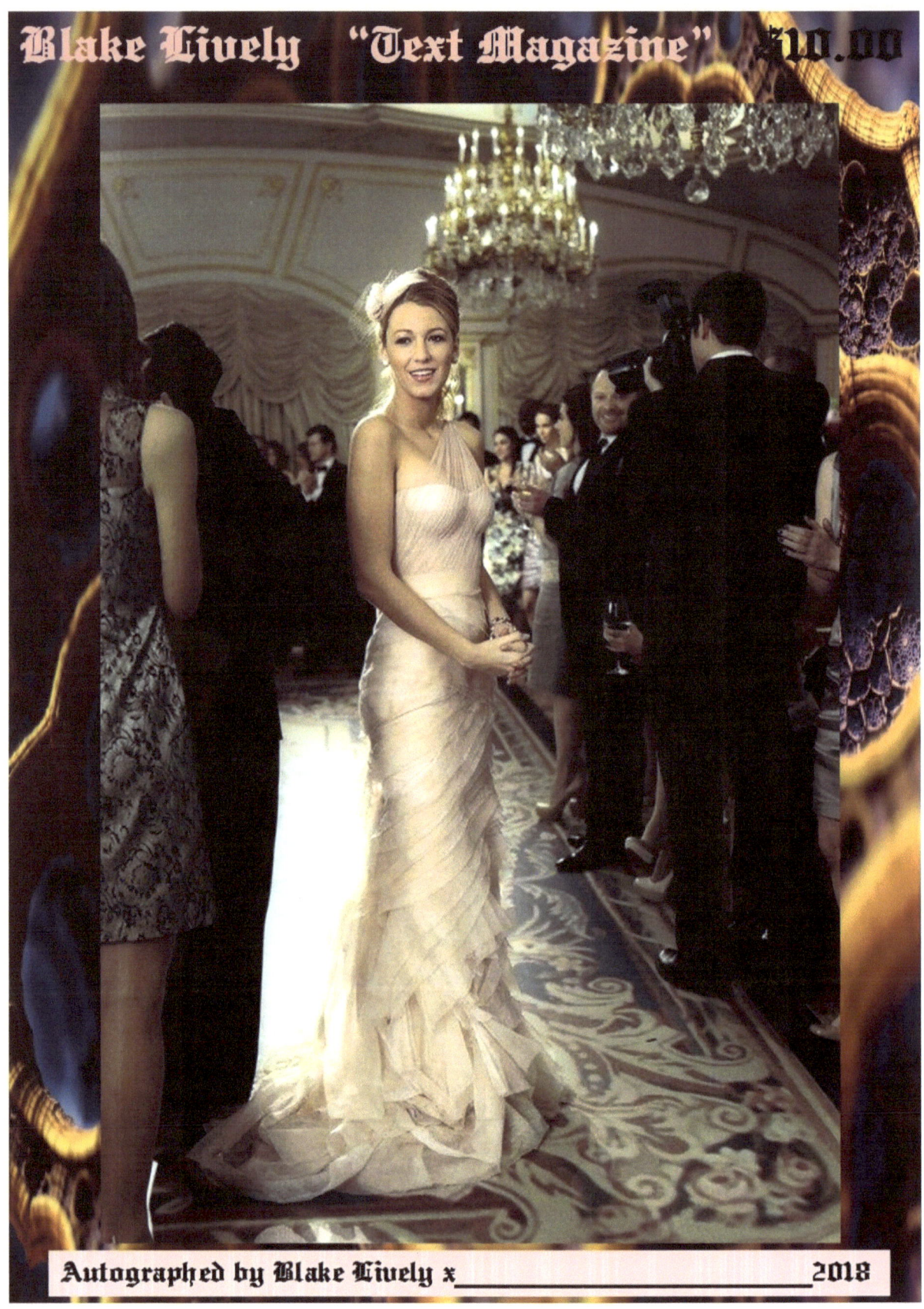

Autographed by Blake Lively x_____ 2018

Blake Lively   "Text Magazine" $10.00

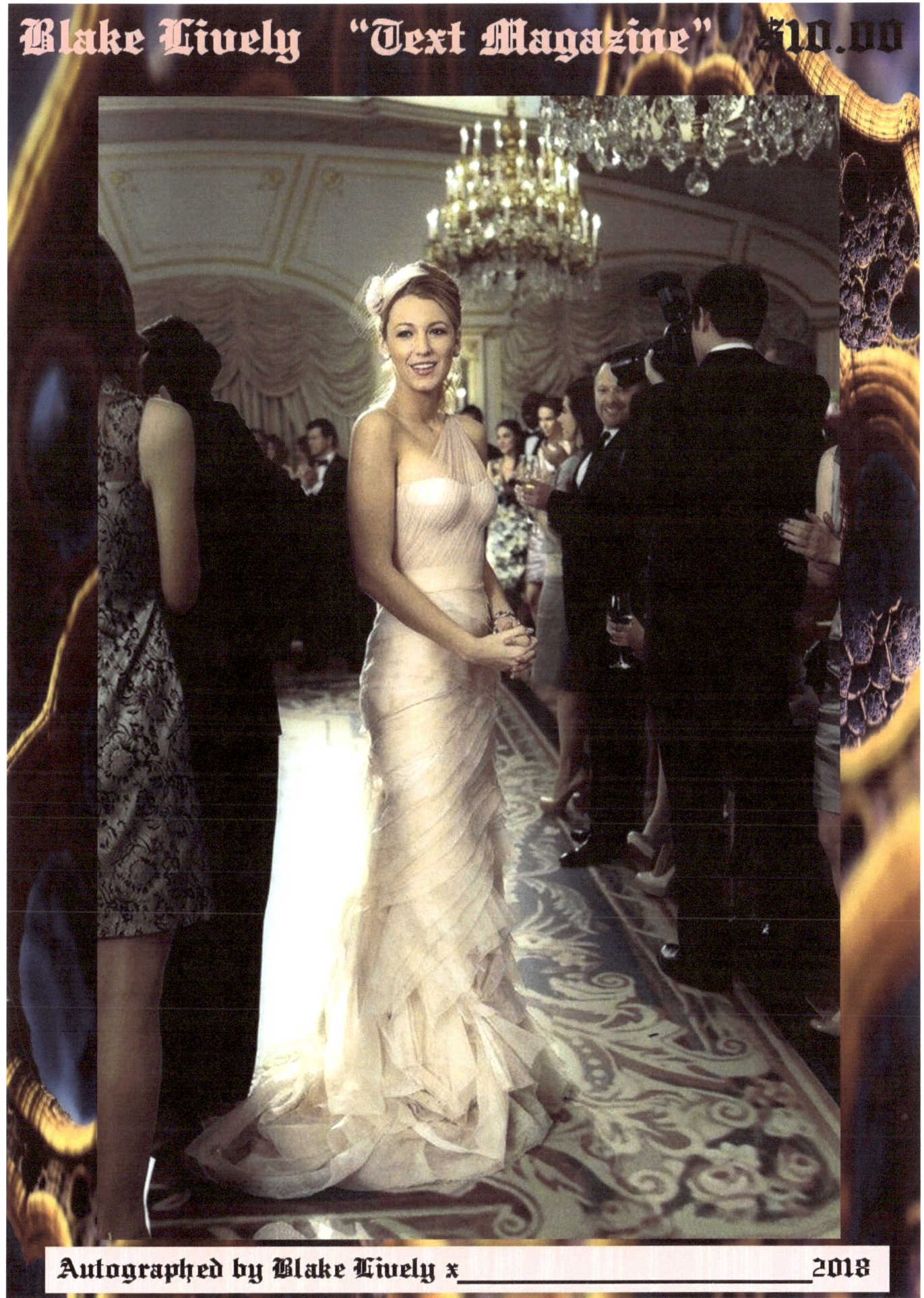

Autographed by Blake Lively x_____ 2018

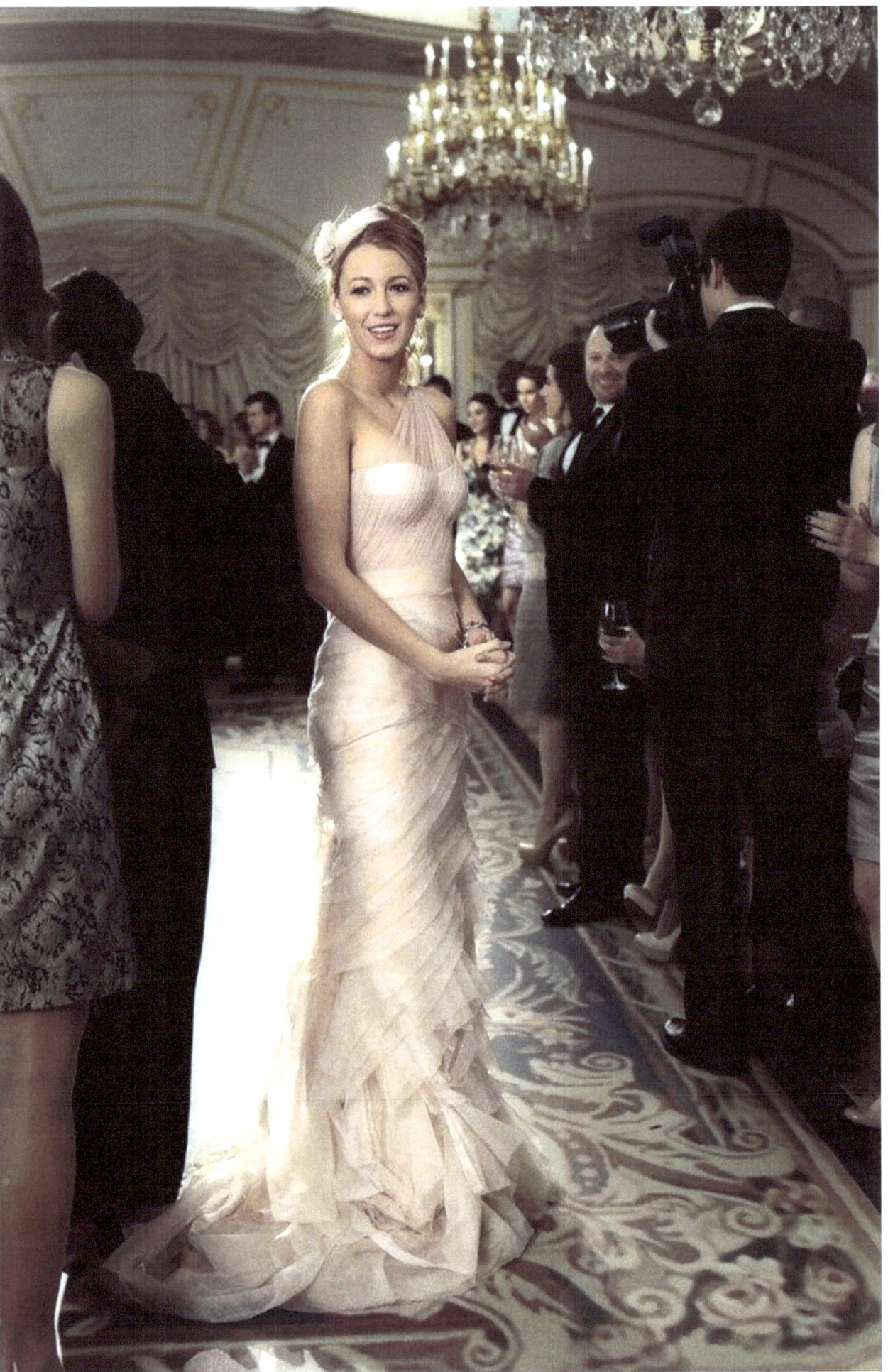

The reiterated conclusion of $40.00 USD an hour, is that this must be a global plan. I repeat the formula of the $2,000.00 dollar Homestead. We first buy one acre of rural property on a wooded lot at the average rate of $1,000.00 an acre. This will alleviate the quick concern of our returning soldiers and other youthful men from thee old Act of 20 acres for $25.00 USD. Now that we have the wooded lot we invest in a chain saw and weed through the scrub wood and sell some of the scrub wood for about $2,000.00 bucks. Leaving the new sum of $2,000.00 dolaros to repay us for the original $1000 dollars invested and giving us enough to buy a fairly new trailer home @ $1,000.00 remodeled. Now we own the property and own the mobile home. There are four other investments to capstone the comfort of home.... one is solar panels on the roof of the trailer, second is a satellite dish, third is a artisan well, and fourth is a Sheepherder Wood / Coal cook stove. Maybe we need to sell more scrub wood, instead of buying things used at sales. Our next investment will be a 30 foot Mess Tent from wholesalers and plant that on one of the four corners of the property, this is for summertime living and creating straight-wood lumber in the Winter months with a felt lining and two canister wood stoves. The lumber will be used in the Spring for building a log cabin in a third corner of the lot. More of the remaining lumber will be used in building a Saltbox home as our showpiece for the property... good to find land with wildlife on the parcel, but as forestry dissipates... since we are rural we can raise small livestock and milk and eggs and gardening as well. Hope you are earning money on your computer now and can afford a foundation for your home and other amenities that come with the average home... documents like this are good, as are photographs and arts and crafts. This $2,000 dollar program seems more expensive... but remember the straight wood also has branches that make quick sales in firewood.

The forty dollars an hour will come... benefits as veterans or other recipients should make it easy to jockey (we can have horses too) about till the flow is liquid and your assets have already just increased too $300,000.00. Not bad at all for a few years of tinkering.

Global Imperialism...
Brought to you by:
pmpbroadcasting@outlook.com,
Signed:
David M Pedjoe

CONFIDENTIALITY

PERSONAL INFORMATION (please print or type)

Your Name: David Michael Pedge
Idea Name: "The Stealth"
Street Address: 21 Cypress Avenue
City: Shrewsbury
State/Prov.: MA
Zip/Postal Code: 01545-1308
Telephone: Residence (508) 845-0042 Business ( ) Same
When is the best time to call? 24/7

BACKGROUND INFORMATION

My Idea for a New Product is...

"The Stealth" Sanitary Napkin Absorbent Pad, Centralized Quilted, by "feather" design Contoured, with "fin" to hold in place.

Creates "Stealth Sanitized"

I came up with my idea when I was...

Studying Toxic Shock Syndrome Back When People Were Dying?

(Roughly Sketch your Idea in this space)

Insert

Inner Absorbency   Quilted Lips

AGREEMENT

I believe, to the best of my knowledge, that I am the original inventor of the idea described herein. I hereby authorize Davison to provide me a no-cost discussion about my idea, with no purchase required. I understand submitting my concept is not a release and that this information cannot be used, disclosed, or sold without my expressed written permission. I also understand that all employees of Davison are required to sign an ethics and confidentiality agreement for my protection. By signing this agreement I understand that Davison does not promise or guarantee any financial gain from the development of any new product or idea.

Client: David M. Pedge   Date: 11/3/04
Client: [signature]   Date: 11/3/04
Acknowledged by: [signature] (Authorized Davison signature)

PLEASE FAX TOLL FREE OR RETURN WHITE COPY IN THE POSTAGE PAID ENVELOPE

Davison, Inc., R&D Park, 595 Alpha Drive, Pittsburgh, PA 15238-2911   Phone: 1-800-54-Ideas   Fax Toll Free: 1-800-540-5490

Dear Super Models:

I have interest once again to reiterate your plans to hold out on nudity, for as long as you can, but certainly before your wallowing in the mire. Being put out to pasture, was a warning my (passed-on) Mom... taught me about to save you girls from rainy-days. My Dad and John Robert Powers Modeling Agency had nothing to do with me as an artisan / photographer. Well there were assets donated to me, by Dad... and once he said your family is with you in spirit. I noted Jacqueline Bouvier was once a JRP girl and models were paid $2,000.00 a shoot. I also offered scholarships to JRP on mine own... so Dad wouldn't go to hell. The payment agreement I read and knew about some twice 90 day deal, that added up to six months before granted payment. But Mom was also a model of wigs and an off-Broadway actress, had me in youth... try out for: "South Pacific" and Ms. Clifford had me as the King in "The Tax King" Play. As I was dressed up a English Lord in a long red jacket and ruffled black shorts and black tights: "I am your King" and vowed to pay you back! This is just a synapsis of my life that led to esteem your progress as I calculated the persona you could attain. It began with "Pink" and the backstage "meet and greet" for $75,000.00 dollars, when the greats only got $20,000.00 for a three day layover in on average NY. NY. and Los Angelus. That dude wasn't driving modeling careers to obsolete annihilation. Therefore I intervened. First with Paula Jones and a $ Million USD kiss. Then I calculated the real results of... what I say again? Well actually it's more than just nudity... it's a three hundred photograph shoot = I can handle 800 photos on my 4 GB San Disk and take the shoot in one day via Jet Blue to Worcester MA. 01602 USA. I will arrange airfare and Hong Kong attire and I'll keep a copy of the photos, only allowing me to create photo story 3 videos with, that I email to you anyways. But you keep the clothes, the camera and the San Disk... then we would allocate the photos into high-definition prints @ $ 3000.00 USD per print, created by publisher and earning income of prints x 800 I would hope. Then being famous (without nudity) you would earn through saturation marketing, as onto Picasso or the price of $ 100,000.00 USD per personally autographed pictures, in an unlimited series, as unto the Farrah Fawcett "pink" bath-suit. That mistakenly had a stamped on signature... that ruined her famed value. Now you know. This should not happen to you. You have evolved as a model, and in demand... as wolves hunger for your, in the buff; composure... still not attained and need it not. The tease, creates a challenge and your haunted by chump-change porn images that disgust you. But if you did, the likes of Esquire your nudity would fetch $ One Billion Dollars! How? Do you know how many magazines would sell? You did the David and Jesus trick? The advertisers would pay big bucks for image in the pages of High-end Markets. You get the copyrights to the image and sell ads and rake in $ One Billion USD for just a few of the business hook-biters. Never mind the magazine itself, and the fact you sold all thee advertisements. Models comprehend this as well as you gentlemen of agreement. Congratulations... your now valued in assets near Two Billion USD. Here's an easy $ 2 Billion for Vanessa Williams = a rebel of tradition. Instant Fame! Instant Gratuities! Fiat!
David M Pedjoe

www.ingramcontent.com/pod-product-compliance
Lightning Source LLC
Chambersburg PA
CBHW040415220526
45473CB00004B/1247